CREATIVE DESIGN IN NEEDLEPOINT LACE

Frontispiece A wall hanging in the Venetian style of
Punto Tagliato a Fogliami, worked by Lady Town.

CREATIVE DESIGN IN NEEDLEPOINT LACE

NENIA LOVESEY

B. T. Batsford Ltd, London

© Nenia Lovesey 1983
First published 1983

ISBN 0 7134 4141 0

Phototypeset by Servis Filmsetting Ltd, Manchester
and printed in Great Britain by
The Pitman Press Ltd
Bath, Somerset
for the publishers
B. T. Batsford Ltd
4 Fitzhardinge Street
London W1H 0AH

Butler & Tanner Ltd,
Frome and London

CONTENTS

Acknowledgements

First my thanks go to Dorothy and Edwin Humphry for all the help they have given me. To Mary Harbard who was brave enough to offer to check the script and to Maureen Walker Lovesey for typing the completed work, as efficiently as they both did in *The Technique of Needlepoint Lace*.

To Rodger Cuthbert who has again produced photographs with the same care and attention to detail as last time. To Pat Gibson, Catherine Barley, Ann Forbes-Cockell, Doreen Holmes, Daphne Keen, Shirley Warren, Mary Anderson, Elsa Took and Heather Neilson for working through the stitches and wheels and for allowing their work to be used to illustrate the book. My thanks also to Lady Town and to Henrietta Curtis, to Phyllis Bradley for working through endless hours of couching. To my long suffering husband who has supplied frames, pillow stands, mounts and anything we have asked for in the way of equipment to get us through the work entailed.

But I, who only seek to keep from being bored,
Am satisfied to live in this my lowly state,
And by my labors grave strive only to create
A gift for womankind, contentment to afford.

Then, ladies, please accept (I pray you will do so)
These patterns and designs I dedicate to you,
To while away your time and occupy your mind.

In this new enterprise there's much that you can learn,
And finally this craft you'll master in your turn.
The work agreeable, the profit great you'll find.

Part of a sonnet 'To the Ladies and Young Misses'
From the book by Federico Vinciolo AD 1587.

The Preparation for Needlepoint

Needlepoint lace is worked on a background material of calico or glazed cotton. Avoid any woollen materials because the tiny hairs in the weave are inclined to become caught up in the lace stitches. The backing has to be at least three times the size of the design, plus turnings all around. First turn in the frayed edges; there is no need to tack edges down at this point, it is usually enough just to run the back of the thumb-nail along the edge. The material is then folded into three, but check that the design is well within the area that is left before going any further. Tack around the three open edges, close to the outside, making short tacking stitches on the working surface. The stitches need not be so short on the back of the material, since they will not become caught up with the needle when working the lace.

The idea of the backing material is to give a firm base on which to work, to avoid puckering. If there is not enough body to the material with the three folds, then use a larger piece and make more folds.

When the lace is finished it is cut away from the design by snipping the stitches of the couched threads between the folds in the backing material as is explained further on in the book. The colour of the base material does not matter, the lace is worked on the design, but do avoid a patterned material.

A small pillow on which to pin the prepared work is useful. It allows two free hands to manipulate the stitches into position and helps keep the work taut. Instructions for making a pillow are given in my book, *The Technique of Needlepoint Lace*. There is also a commercially made pillow; the address is given in the list of suppliers at the end of this book. The work should be pinned to the pillow at the top and bottom as it has to be lifted and rearranged to suit the direction of the stitches. A knitting needle or chop stick is pushed between the backing material and the pillow and the lace stitches are worked on the ridge formed; this allows leverage to the needle. The pillow is essential when working with fine threads, but with any threads up to the equivalent of 100 crochet cotton it is not important.

LAYING THE CORDONNET

Before starting to lay the cordonnet, study the design to see how far the threads can be laid without having to cut off and rejoin. The cordonnet is always worked as a pair of threads laid side by side around the design.

To start, take twice the length of thread required, fold in half and the first couch stitch is taken through the loop of the fold. Both threads are then couched together as far as possible along the design. On reaching a point where there is a spur off the main run of the design, leave one thread behind. The other thread of the pair is taken along the spur, held at the end with a couching stitch and then folded back on itself and couched back into its partner. The two threads continue side by side along the design until it is necessary to use just the one thread again.

At any point where the couched threads pass one of these spurs, on a return journey for instance, pass one or both threads through the little loop formed by the fold. In this way all parts of the design are locked together and there is no fear of the lace coming apart when taken off the backing material.

If using coloured threads for working the lace, use the same colour of sewing silk to couch with. Use fine-pointed needles for the couching and make sure the thread is taken through all layers of the backing material. The reason for this is that once the lace is finished, the couching stitches are cut between the layers of material, and the work just lifts off. The little cut ends of the couching can

An eighteenth-century piece worked in the shape of an oval, depicting a lady on horseback.

then be pulled out of the lace at the back. Some threads do get caught in the lace stitches and have to be cut close to the work. If the same colour has been used the little cut ends will not show.

If a new thread has to be joined in, leave the short thread out and lay a new thread in its place beside the other original thread. Make four or five couching stitches, then pull the new thread gently through until the end is just secured under the stitches; continue to lay the original one of the pair with the new thread. Never let both threads run out close together; always allow at least 2 inches (5 cm) of new thread to run alongside an existing thread.

When reaching the end of the design, take one thread through the loop made in the fold of the thread at the start, fold it over on itself and whip it back to the two laid threads for about an inch (2.5 cm). Take the couching thread through the backing, make it secure and cut off. The other

thread of the pair is continued over the pair at the start of the design, whipped as before and the couching thread is taken through the backing and finished off. The two ends of the laid thread are now cut off as close as possible.

At no point from now on does the working thread go through the backing material. When starting the lace work, run the working thread through three or four couching stitches to where the filling or ground is to start. Lay the working thread under the thumb and make a buttonhole stitch, taking the needle under the couched threads and over the new working thread; this forms a knot (see Fig. 1).

The work is finished in the same way. Take the working thread through three or four couching stitches and make a knot stitch. All new threads start and end this way.

STARTING A PROJECT

Prepare a drawing or if using this design trace off on to white paper, cover with acetate film and tack to the prepared backing material. Acetate

8

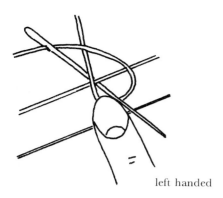

left handed

Fig. 1 Knot stitch.

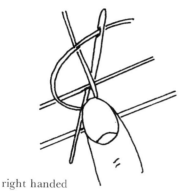

right handed

the design lies at the back; try to lay this part of the cordonnet first and build up to the areas that appear toward the front. Always remember to join the threads wherever they pass each other, either by going through the loops as given in the instructions for laying the cordonnet or by making a knot stitch. It is important that all parts of the design are joined together before starting the lace work. Remember the cordonnet is the framework of the lace, and the couching threads are only for keeping this framework in position while the lace is being worked. It is important that the couching threads are secure at the start and end of all new threads.

film can be found at most drawing office suppliers and it is a transparent film with an adhesive backing. It can be had with either a gloss or matt finish, the matt finish being better if working under artificial light as there is no reflection from it. Blue or green are the best colours if working with white threads and colourless or pale yellow when working with dark threads.

Always use a ball-point sewing needle for working the stitches to prevent the splitting of threads. The needles are made by Millwards and Singers and can be purchased at most department stores and needlework shops. They are made purposely for use with stretch fabrics and although tapestry needles will do if the ball-points prove hard to find, the eyes of these needles are meant to take wool and are too clumsy for most lace work.

Carefully read through the instructions for laying the cordonnet. Then decide which part of

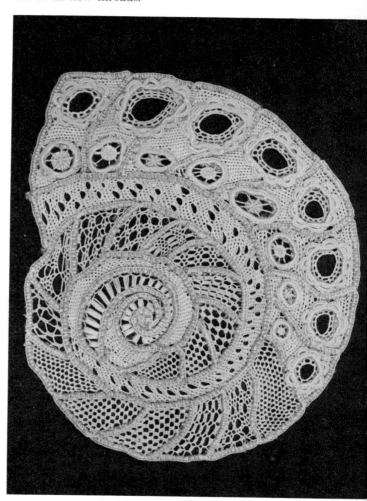

A cross section of a nautilus shell worked by Pat Gibson as a sampler, using the stitches given in this book and in *The Technique of Needlepoint Lace*.

9

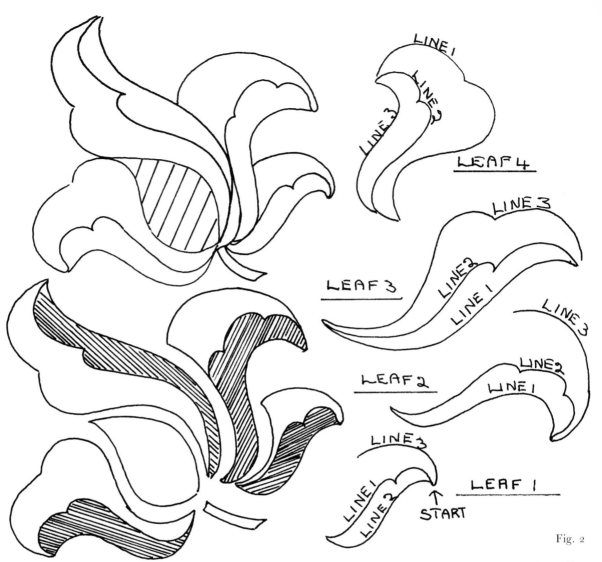

Fig. 2

Fig. 2 shows four leaves or petals with an oval centre, plus a small stalk. Each leaf consists of two parts. The shaded areas are the bottom sections of the leaves in each case and each leaf is numbered. In the drawing, each line of the leaves is numbered; the cordonnet should be laid along these lines in the following order. Couch each thread or threads as follows:

Leaf no. 1

Start at the top of line 1 with a length of thread folded in two and bring the first of the couch stitches up through the loop formed; lay the two threads on the line and couch down to the base. Fold the two threads over onto themselves and continue along the lower line marked 2. On reaching the tip of the leaf, take one thread through the loop formed where the thread was folded in half and continue along the line marked 3 to where it joins leaf no. 2.

Leaf no. 2

Drop one thread and couch the single thread to the top of the leaf along line 1, couching down all the way and making sure it is secure at the tip of the leaf. Fold over onto itself and pass the needle through the couching stitches. There is now a double thread couched from the tip of the leaf down to where the second thread was left behind. Pick up this thread and continue with both

10

threads down to the base and connect to the first leaf. Fold these over as before and continue up the line numbered 2, through the loop at the top, then along line 3 to the point where it meets leaf no. 3.

Leaf no. 3

This is worked in the same way and in the same order as leaf no. 2, up to the tip with the single thread, back down the line to where the two leaves connect; then pick up the second thread and continue down to the base. Make sure this leaf is securely fixed to the others at the base. Now work up line 2 through the loop at the tip and back down line 3.

Leaf no. 4

Continue around the bottom of the oval and up line 1. Take one thread through two or three couching stitches of leaf no. 3 where this leaf touches, then on to the tip. Secure firmly at the top, then back down line 2. Drop one thread and couch along line 3 with the single thread, go through the loop at the tip, fold over and run the needle through the couching stitches at the base; secure to the other leaves. Then with both threads go down one side of the stalk and back up to the other side. The point where the stalk and the base of all the leaves meets will be covered by a couronne; instructions for these will be found further on in the book.

In a lot of the old laces very few different stitches were used. An openwork area would be surrounded by a solid filling, while the enclosed parts of a design, sometimes called a casket, would be given a different treatment. The lined area in the centre of the design could be a casket in this piece of lace. A better idea of how a casket is formed will be seen in the chapter on designing.

Two openwork fillings placed side by side not only lose their effect, they also become a weak point as there is no body to the finished lace. Another point to bear in mind is that if the fillings are used on an outside edge, the shape could be lost through constant handling.

With the design given here, all the shaded parts need a corded stitch to hold the shape. The other parts of the leaves can have any of the fillings given in this book or others shown in *The Technique of Needlepoint Lace*. When starting or joining in a new thread run the needle under three or four couching stitches and make a knot stitch at the point where the row of stitches is to start. The

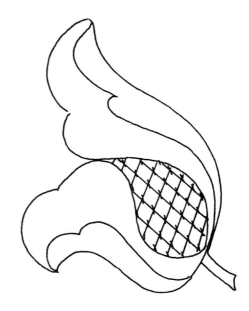

Fig. 3
The centre of the design using a square mesh.

same thing happens in reverse when ending a thread: make a knot stitch at the end of the row, then run the needle through the couching stitches and cut off. All the cut ends are well covered once the cordonnette is laid.

For working the fillings it is best to start along the longest edge of the area being filled. As the rows of the fillings are being worked, the stitches appear to arc in the middle of the rows. When the last row is being worked, take the needle under the cordonnet as each stitch is worked; this brings the rows of stitches into straight lines. Work the corded stitches first, because the density of the stitches and the rows gives a firm base on which to anchor the filling stitches.

The centre of the design can be worked in any of the fillings using a square mesh (Fig. 3). The Point d'Angleterre wheel filling would be the right size stitch for this space. Details for working the stitch can be found in chapter 7, on fillings, along with Katie's kisses or Elecia filling which would also be suitable.

Once all the areas have been worked, the design is ready to receive the cordonnette. Do wait until this part of the procedure is finished before discarding your first piece of work; laying the cordonnette will improve it beyond recognition.

Raised Work

In the past, in order to give lace a three-dimensional finish, a cord, made up of a number of threads, was laid around the outline of all sections of the lace. This cord was then either couched or, in the more luxurious laces, was buttonholed over the entire length. Often picots were added in great profusion, so small that it is almost impossible to see them with the naked eye. White horsehair was added to give the lace much more body. If using horsehair, always wash it and leave to dry under pressure to stop the hair crimping. It can be wrapped in paper towels and laid under a pile of books.

Start to lay the cordonnette with two or more threads of the same colour as the lace and cover with buttonhole stitches, the ridge edge facing outwards from the centre of the work. After five or six stitches have been worked, pull the laid threads through gently, until the ends of the threads disappear under the stitches just worked. Continue to buttonhole over these threads until reaching a point where it needs to be thicker, such as working around a curve along an outside edge.

To work the extra threads, lay them alongside the others already being worked, make five or six stitches over the original and the new threads, then gently pull through until the new ends disappear under the buttonhole stitches just made. When the need to reduce the threads arises cut off one or two threads, make a few stitches, then cut off more as necessary. On reaching the base of the design, work over two or three threads only, then add in again as the design calls for a wider edge.

To finish the project the cordonnette is laid in the same working order as the cordonnet was couched for the foundation. Line 1 of the first leaf could have more padding than lines 2 and 3. This will lift that line and make it look nearer.

The same applies for line 2 of leaf no. 2. Leaf no.

3 should have the top curve of line 2 lifted, then follow over the top and down line 3 just as far as the first curve.

Line 2 of leaf no. 4 needs to be thickened over the first and second curve, thinning out as it reaches the base.

The whole design should, by now, have taken on a new look, only waiting for the finishing touches of a couronne. To remove the work, snip the couch threads between the two layers of backing material, lift the lace and pull out any threads of the couch stitches that remain. Threads that have been caught in the working of the lace need to be sheared off carefully.

THE USE OF COURONNES

Couronnes were used for the final decoration of the finished lace. They were the feature of Venetian lace, originally called *Punto Tagliato a Fogliami*, which is now called Raised Point.

Some of the old laces stand in double and treble relief and were described as *Scolpito in Relievo*. The scrolls and rings are made separately and are sewn in position after the lace is taken from the backing material. They are attached with small stab stitches through the lace, usually at the centres of flowers or at the base of a design where a number of different fillings meet. They come in all shapes and sizes, plain or ornamented with picots, and are quite often made up of more than one layer.

It will be necessary to have either a number of different sized knitting needles or to buy a special ring stick. The ring sticks are of highly polished hard wood, made especially for lace, and are graded down from a large diameter at the top, to a very small diameter at the bottom; the supplier's name is at the back of the book. The easiest way to find the size of couronne needed for any particular area is to lay the ring stick over the centre to be filled. The sides of the ring stick must be within the

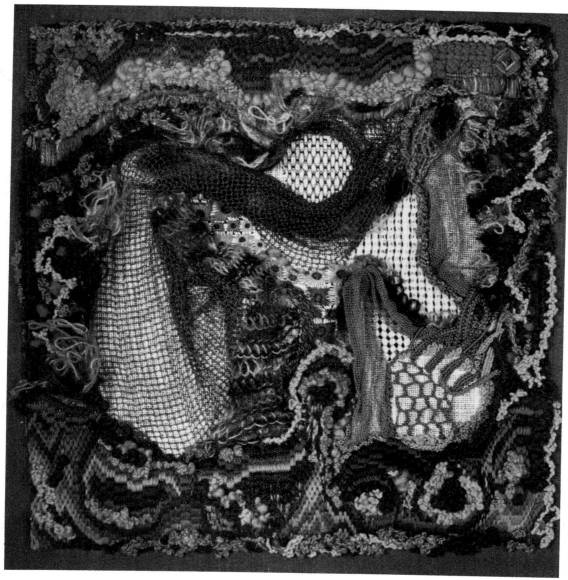

circle of this centre. Allow for the thickness of the padding that is formed by the wrapping of the thread around the stick, plus the buttonhole stitches that make the ring. When making the very ornate ones with loops and picots the centre ring has to be smaller. If the ring turns out to be too big, do not discard it; make a smaller one and add on top of the first making a double tier.

The basic ring that forms the simplest couronne is the one to try first, and will give some idea of the amount of padding needed to make a substantial

This design was taken from the Kent Caves in Torquay, Devon, and worked by the author using techniques incorrectly called needlepoint. *From top:* Canvas work used out of context because so many people call it needlepoint, when in reality it started life as Gros point, petit point, Berlin wool work, working down through drawn thread, pulled thread, netting, true needlepoint and padded canvas work at the base.

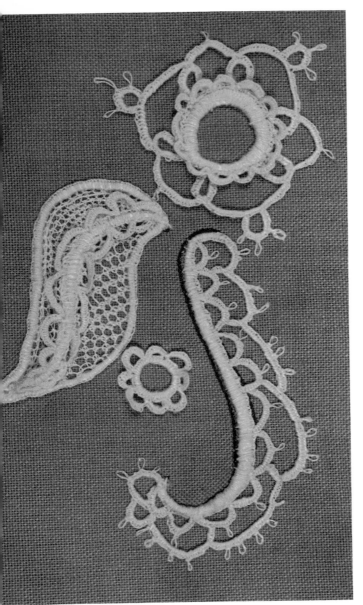

Couronnes worked on a ring stick and some worked directly on a laid cordonet.

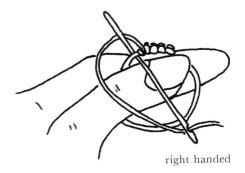

right handed

Fig. 4

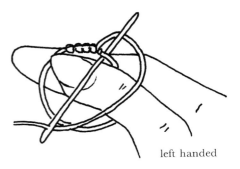

left handed

The needle needs a long length of thread and the end is wrapped around the end of the ring stick a number of times, at the desired diameter. The greater the number of rounds, the thicker the finished ring. Slip the needle under all the threads while still on the stick and make the first buttonhole stitch. Once this first stitch is made, gently force the wrapping threads down the stick, but before taking off the very end hold between finger and thumb and make some more buttonhole stitches before letting go.

It is often easier to work away from you, that is, putting the needle into the loop and forming the buttonhole stitch on the outside (Fig. 4). When the threads are all covered, take the needle through the buttonhole stitches first made, along at the back of the ring. Make a note at this stage of the size of the ring used to wrap the threads around, how many times the thread was wrapped

ring. Having made two or three different size rings, make a note of how many stitches were needed to fill the entire circle. It will be found that half-way around the ring the stitches can be pushed closer together to make sure the stitches really are well packed in.

around the ring stick, just how many stitches were needed to fill the ring and the size of thread used. It all proves very useful information later.

The next one to try is a looped one. For this example we will work on a ring of fifteen stitches, with five loops around the outside. Having worked this ring it will be easy to organize any number of stitches into equal distances between loops.

Wrap the thread around the ring stick and make the first stitch to hold, then work another three stitches. Take the needle through the loop at the top of the first stitch made, now take it back and through the top of the fourth stitch on the ring. Now back and through the first stitch once again. There are now four stitches on the ring and three loose loops over the top of them. Over these three loops work as many buttonhole stitches as is needed to cover completely. This brings the working thread back to the top of the fourth stitch on the ring.

Now work three stitches over the ring and take the working thread back over the top of these stitches through the top of the fourth stitch and make another three loops in the same way. Keep the loops all the same size and use the same number of stitches to cover the loop. Make three more stitches over the ring and make the loops back into the seventh stitch covering the loops with the same number of buttonhole stitches as before.

Make three more stitches over the ring and make the three loops back over into the tenth stitch, cover as before. Only two stitches are now needed on the ring to make the fifteen stitches intended in the first count. The working thread goes through the first stitch where the first loop started and back into the thirteenth stitch; make the three loops and cover with the correct number of buttonhole stitches to finish off the final loop. The couronne will have fifteen stitches on the ring, five loops each with the same number of buttonhole stitches; hopefully each loop will be the same size and there should be two stitches on the ring between each set of loops.

Not all couronnes are made on a ring stick; they can be formed directly onto the cordonnet. Venetian laces from the early sixteenth century show the use of the added refinement of scallops worked into the laid threads. The scallops were worked in double and treble layers with picots along the entire length.

DESIGNING FOR LACE

There are two trains of thought when designing for needlepoint lace. One is that of the traditionalist, the other is the modern approach.

The arabesque Spanish shapes can be accommodated into very modern designs, the intertwined foliage and curved shapes lend themselves extremely well to the sculptured ornament of Couronnes. This kind of designing is especially good for place mats, under paperweights, for box tops or for being used to make yardage for underwear or other types of clothing or household goods. Another good source of ideas for the traditionalist is from Jacobean embroidery. These designs are usually of flowers and foliage and were very much in vogue during the period of James I at the beginning of the seventeenth century. This was also the time when needlepoint lace was almost at its peak. The best designs originated on the European continent, but changes in fashion moved very slowly, with one period overlapping another. What was high fashion in France could take years to become popular in another country. For this reason, designs in lace appear to have followed the culture of the country in which the lace was made.

The modern representation has a much wider choice, from the entirely visual aspect to the great many shapes that can be found in the wonderful world seen through a microscope. Beautiful white frost patterns can be found in the garden on a winter morning after an extremely severe night. Vegetable markets are an unexpected source for design. The crates of vegetables and exotic fruits have medallions with exporters' names or seals stamped on them, which seem to burst from them like seeds from a pod. Some of the symbols and numbers from the Far East make the most exciting shapes. There is design everywhere if your eyes are trained to look for the unusual.

Designing for a specific shape is straightforward enough if one knows the easy way to go about it. Most first pieces of lace are small, in fact the very first piece to come off the backing material is looked upon in horror. But never throw this first piece away, keep it in a file to compare with the next piece and always work the first design twice. The starting and ending of rows can be compared, the direction of the stitches could suggest that they should have been worked at a different angle, a finer thread might have been better or the stitches needed to have been made smaller, closer or larger. All these things are there before you in your first piece of lace. It is there for you to see and improve upon instead of guesswork and any mistakes can be rectified in the second piece. So this next effort is going to be a masterpiece and is to be framed or is going under a paperweight for posterity. So let us be sure the size and the design, meant to be square, or round, or even a little of both so it needs to be an oval, are right before the work starts. The design needs to fill an area; too small and it is lost in the expanse of background, too big and the edges are lost behind the frame. Box lids, picture frames and paperweights all have a lip that holds the glass or where the backing is stuck, so the shape must fit in the area that shows.

The easiest way to draw a circle is to use a compass. But if there is a schoolboy in the family, the day Mother wants to use a compass Son is doing technical drawing at school and the compass just happens to be with him.

There is one way, that of using circular graph paper. It is sold as a Graph Data Pad, is an A4 size, either cartridge or tracing paper. The tracing paper is the most suitable in this case.

There are thirty-six sections to each circle,

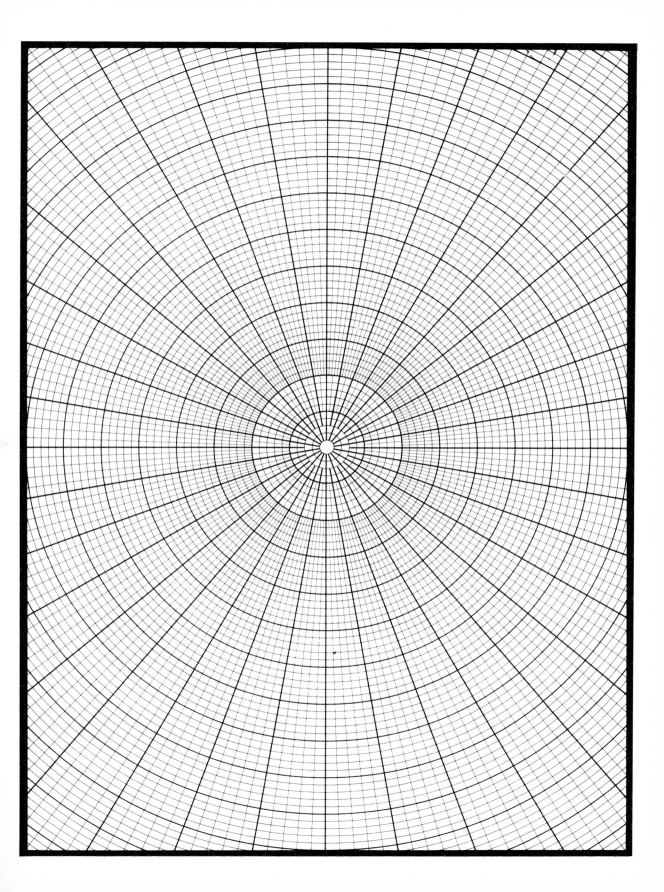

which can be broken down as follows:

Every other section equals 18 repeats
3 sections = 12 repeats
4 sections = 9 repeats
6 sections = 6 repeats
$8\frac{1}{2}$ sections = 4 repeats
or the 12 sections can become one third of the circle.

Circle the ring to the size needed and divide it into the number of sections required. Place a piece of tracing paper over the ring and trace off the section to be used, so that you work only on this wedge to form the design. Fold the wedge in half and draw half the design to the fold. Turn over and trace off the other half of the design. If the drawing is held against the window pane, it is easy to follow the trace with the light behind the first half. Make the number of copies required, i.e. 12,

9, 6, etc., and arrange in a circle, lay under the sectional paper and draw up the complete design.

A circle can still be formed without the aid of graph paper or compass. Take a square of paper and fold into a triangle, now fold again to form another triangle half the size. Make both of these folds again to make sixteen folds. Cut in a very slight curve from the lowest edge of the paper which will be opposite the fold of the wedge. To be very sure of the circle, measure the length of the shortest edge from the point up, then mark up the same length on the folded edge and cut off to these marks. If the cut is made with a pronounced curve the circle, when opened up, will be scalloped. When the paper is opened, there will be sixteen clear folds and the design is worked to these sections in the same way as given for the graph paper.

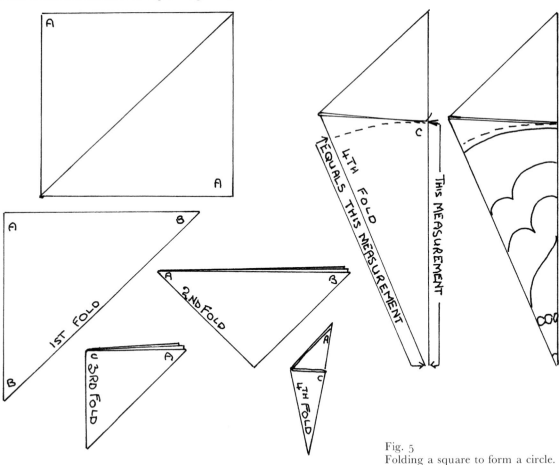

Fig. 5
Folding a square to form a circle.

Fig. 6

Brugge-type mat; a circle using four repeats and a
central motif worked by the author.

Fig. 7a

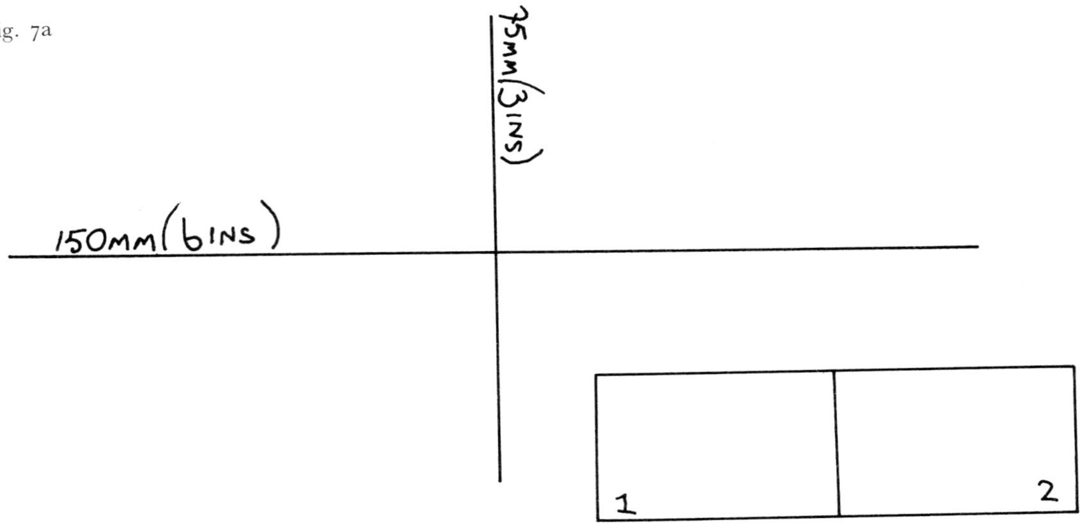

b

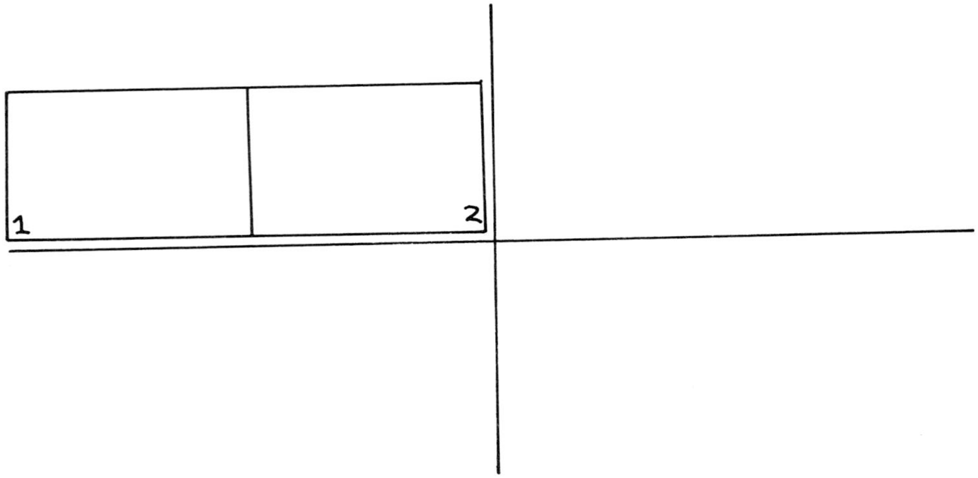

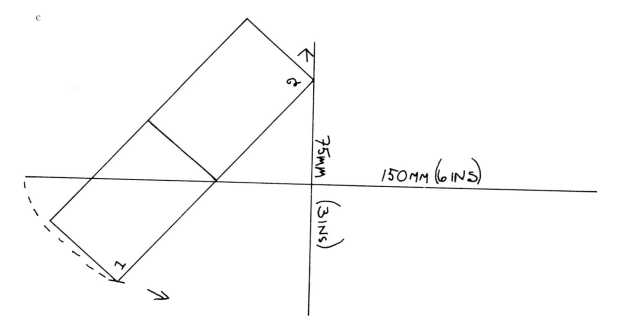

c

2

75mm
(3 INS)

150MM (6 INS)

1

To form an oval, decide on the length and width needed and for this exercise the proposed size will be 6 × 3 inches (150 × 75 mm). Draw a straight line 6 inches (150 mm) in length. At right angles and directly through the centre of this line draw a 3 inch (75 mm) line and mark this line off into equal sections about $\frac{1}{10}$ inch (3 mm) apart (Fig. 7a).

Take a separate piece of paper, fold to exactly the same size as the 3 inch (75 mm) line on the drawing. Mark the two corners on the lower edge 1 and 2 and mark the centre. Place the separate paper on the left-hand half of the long line on the drawing, with corner 2 at the centre, touching the upright line (Fig. 7b). Keep the centre mark travelling along the 6 inch (150 mm) line and mark off points or divisions at corner 1.

When 2 reaches the top of the vertical and 1 reaches the bottom of it, one quarter of the oval has been formed. Join the marks made at 1 into a continuous line. The rest of the oval can then be traced off, by first folding along the 6 inch (150 mm) line and then folding along the vertical line. If it is not convenient to fold the drawing, turn the separate piece of paper upside down, take the corner marked 1 down the central vertical line, keep the central line along the horizontal line and the corner marked 2 will form the top quarter of the oval. To draw the other half, place 1 to the centre vertical line and as 1 travels up this line, 2 will chart the bottom right-hand corner. Turn the paper upside down as before, then as 2 travels down the vertical line 1 will form the top right-hand quarter (Fig. 7c).

A square will be correct if the first line is drawn over the length needed, first butting the end of the ruler along the straight edge of the paper. Make sure the edge touches all the way; if one corner of the ruler is out fractionally the line will tilt. Make the second line, butting the ruler against the first drawn line, draw the other two lines in the same way. Do check that the end of the ruler is straight before you start, or the square will be far from right. If Son has not taken the T-square, then it would be easier to use that, but I am talking from experience.

Fig. 8

Once the shape is determined and the size is right, the next step is to get the design to fit. With the circle, refold the piece of paper that has been cut to size and use just one section. If a scroll design is made using just this one section of the ring, working from the point to the outside edge and touching both sides, it will be enough to fill the circle. Take a tracing of the scroll just drawn and lay it under each section in turn.

Fold the oval template in half, then into quarters, make the design with the curved edge at the top and the point of the wedge at the bottom. Fill the area with a drawing from the top to the bottom in a fan shape.

The square can be folded into quarters or eighths. Work from the outside to the middle. For both the oval and the square, the drawing is transferred to the other areas, by taking the tracing, either on its own or as a mirror image.

Fig. 10 shows a square with four different woven wheels and four fillings. The centre leaves are connected with Ardenza bars, the bars connecting the tops of the leaves to the outside edge are buttonholed with a central picot. The outside edge is worked in whipped stitch.

Fig. 9

Fig. 10

Fig. 11

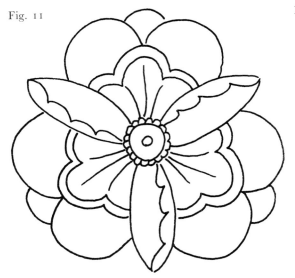

Fig. 12

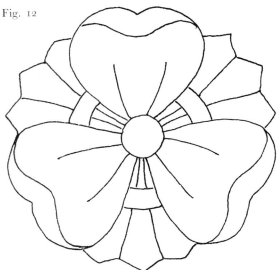

These two designs (Figs 11 & 12) use one third of a circle for each repeat worked over twelve sections of the circular graph paper. Once the design is worked, lay the cordonnette over the back three sections first, then lay a thicker cordonnette for the petals to lift them away from the rest of the design.

The central wheels are worked using a ring stick to form the core, which is then buttonholed around and attached after the motif is taken from the backing material.

The wheels can be left plain or can have scallops or picots worked around the outside edge.

Fig. 13

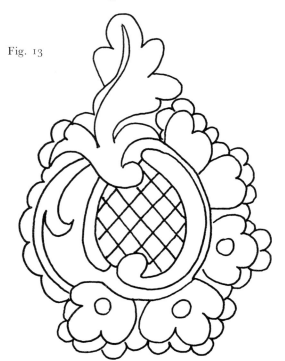

This design (Fig. 13) would work into a commercial pattern for a collar or tie-ends on a blouse. Alsace 60 lace thread is the right weight of thread if using cotton or 130/3 for silk.

The centre was intended for the Bruges filling and the outside flower shapes can be worked in the Genoa lace stitch or the pea variation. The scalloped edge gives a firm finish.

Worked as tie-ends on a blouse in muted shades of lavenders and petrol blues, by Pat Gibson.

Fig. 14a

b

This design (Fig. 14a & b) has been taken from an old Spanish lace. One section has been taken out of context and mirror imaged to use as an alternative to the last design. Both designs could be used in series to form the whole of a collar or used just as ends. This lace was worked in the following stitches, starting from the scrolls at the base; these have rows of corded stitch top and bottom and little rings formed over a figure of eight foundation through the centre. The next space up was worked in fine mesh, while the space above that was worked in Spanish ground. The central motif is in corded stitch, with a light mesh in the centre. The divided section is worked in alternating fine and heavier weight threads in a fairly close mesh and the outside edge is worked in close buttonhole stitch over a cordonnette.

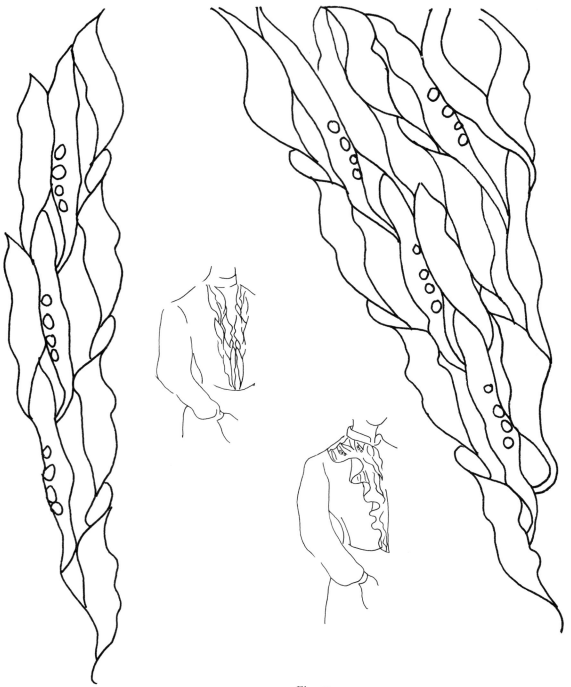

Fig. 15
Laburnum seed pods used as a design for the front
or (right) sleeves of a blouse. Designed and drawn
by Shirley Warren.

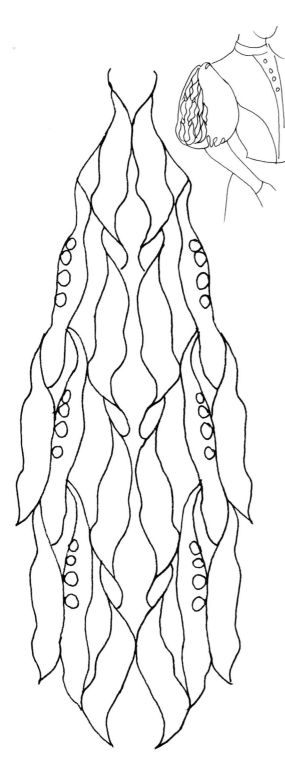

REPETITION

The best and by far the easiest way to construct a design for lace edging is to work on graph paper with cut-out shapes. Two motifs can be butted together into a straight edge, with the centres of each motif given a different filling to stop the whole thing becoming too monotonous. Three motifs give a more interesting design, because often the spaces left between the shape make yet another motif. Play on light and shade, making sure that the corded areas of two motifs when placed together do not become too heavy. Various shapes can be connected by a series of curves, set at the same angle, which will allow each repeat to stay on a straight edge. Along the width of the graph paper draw a line which must be touched by the lowest point of each repeat. Draw another line to be the guide for the top edge of the lace. Lace does not have to stay as a straight edge either top or bottom, but when drawing an edging the top and bottom straight lines keep the design uniform.

Take two motifs and an arc to experiment with, then, when the flow of the design is established, other motifs can be added if necessary to widen the lace. Each block made by the three motifs becomes a repeat pattern, so the arc must be placed in such a position that it brings the other motifs of the second block in line for each repeat. Cut out the three motifs (Fig. 17), draw the top and bottom lines on the graph paper, then arrange and rearrange the motifs between the two lines until quite satisfied that it is a pleasing pattern. Cut small pieces of sellotape, fold in half to make a hinge, then stick to the back of each shape and into position on the graph paper. Lay tracing paper over the design and trace off. Having done this, lay the traced design next to the original. It should lie at the same degree, with the same points touching the top and bottom lines drawn on the graph paper. The tracing and the shapes may have to be moved slightly to bring them in line or a bar can be added to connect if a space appears between the repeats. Once these two blocks lie correctly, so will the repeats.

The motifs will each be worked separately, then brought together to form the blocks. Once these blocks are together, each is added to the last to form the length needed. Decide how long the lace is to be, then add up the number of repeats needed. If the lace is to be worked around the bottom of a nightdress or something similar, it

Fig. 16

Fig. 17

often works better to measure the repeats and make the lace to the nearest measurement called for, then either to increase or decrease the width of the garment to suit the lace. If doing this makes too much difference, lay the lace evenly around the hem, making the back central. Then design something to lay centre front, either widen the repeat pattern, or, if there is less room to play with, see if the design will stand up from the hem, starting at the widest point and trailing off to a point where the design can be broken.

Having decided how many repeats are needed, count the number of individual motifs of each design (Figs 18–20). Draw them up separately and mount them under the acetate film and onto backing material. If using three different motifs there will be three different backing materials to work on; by ringing the changes and working on the three designs in turn, there is no likelihood of becoming bored with the whole thing. Each individual motif works up quickly, whereas a repeat pattern of 6 inches (150 mm) would take longer. The motifs are joined together before laying the cordonnette and in this case it is better to join in blocks of one repeat, as this is easier to handle. As each repeat is finished, it is added to

the previous one. To do this, butt together, making sure they are in line, and tack to backing material. The joining thread is kept close to the knot of the buttonhole stitches of the cordonnette. It is not necessary to go through every stitch of the cordonnette but the closer the stitches are worked the less likelihood there is of them showing.

If designing for a wedding veil or anything that has a set length, start from the two bottom corners. First design a pattern in the form of a triangle and draw a mirror image. To do this make the first drawing, then turn it over, lay a sheet of tracing paper over the blank side, hold up to a window and trace off the design. The two drawings will then be turned toward each other. These will have to be fairly large or they will be inconspicuous from a distance, so aim for an overall design of 10 inches (250 mm) in length and the same in height. Now infill for at least the same distance along the bottom of the design, using either two or three scrolls interlaced with bows, or a series of small rose sprays and leaves (Figs 21–24). This will cover about 40 inches (100 cm) of hem. Then butt the two corners together to form a triangle which will lie central to the hem to give another 20 inches (510 mm) and fill in with

28

Fig. 18

Fig. 19

Fig. 20

29

The Fire Ball embroidery shows the use of colour shading.

A repeat of Fig. 18 worked in 100/35 silk, suggesting a range of stitches.

the scrolls or sprays. If necessary, break the scrolls up with a smaller version of the central design.

The two side edges can be sprinkled with small sprays, scrolls and individual motifs, getting smaller toward the top. Do not take a heavy design too close to the top, as this prevents the veil from falling in soft folds, where it lies under the head-dress. Small flowers or bows can be applied at random over the whole area, but it will depend on how heavy the main design appears.

Figs 25 and 26 on page 34 show three different floral shapes which have been arranged within the two halves of the collar and cuffs of a commercial blouse pattern. The flowers and leaves need to be worked in a heavier weight thread than the connecting bars and the scalloped edge. The collar is of the Peter Pan type, which could be used for either a front or back opening.

Fig. 27 on page 35 shows a design taken from an early eighteenth century handkerchief. The ground is almost entirely made of Bride's Picotees, which are bars that have a scallop each side of the centre and each scallop has two picots worked into

it. The deep curve within the elongated flower shape and the corner between the scroll and the pomegranate is worked in a fine double Brussels stitch.

The pomegranate and all the leaves and small flowers are worked in corded stitch, while the elongated flower has the four-hole diamond worked into the curves at the end of each petal. If the Bride's Picotee sounds too daunting, the whole design can be mounted into fine net, the net being cut away at the edge of the design. This same design can be seen in the photograph of the chalice veil on page 134.

COLOUR AND THE EMBROIDERER
Lace methods can be used in conjunction with embroidery in many different ways. The smoke that surrounds the 'Fire Ball' embroidery (see page 34) is worked in Brussels stitch in three shades of grey stranded cotton, while the raised areas are

Fig. 21

Fig. 22

Fig. 23

Fig. 24

Fig. 25

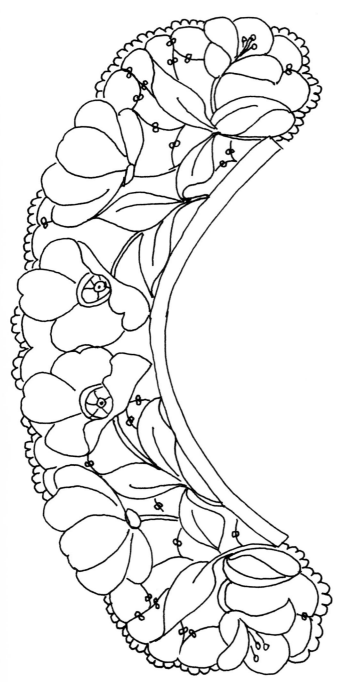

Fig. 26

worked in corded stitch around cottonwool balls and beads in stranded cotton and crochet cotton.

Colour changes can be abrupt or gradual, depending on the effect needed. The ideal stitches for shading are the corded stitches, and a whole range of tones can be worked with just three or four colours. Those who have not had experience in colour mixing might find the following information useful. A hue is a colour in its natural form; if white is added to that colour it becomes a tint; if black is added it becomes a shade of the true colour. All hues, tints, and shades are tones of colour, depending on how light or dark the colour is in relation to white or black.

The easiest form of shading is with stranded cotton, which is formed from six strands of thread. It will need a colour and a grey. All greys vary according to the colours in their make-up, so choose a grey that is based on the hue that is being used. For example, blue/grey when using red/blues, a green/grey when using green/blues,

yellow/grey for orange/pinks and red/grey for scarlet/purples.

The following tables are useful. Use three strands of thread for both the cording and the buttonhole stitches and work two or three rows between each colour change. Start by using the pure colour for both the cording and the buttonhole stitch.

BUTTONHOLE STITCHES		CORDING	
Main Colour	Grey/White	Main Colour	Grey/White
3	0	3	0
3	0	2	1
3	0	1	2
2	1		3
1	2		3
	3		3

Changing from one tone of colour to another, for example from pink to maroon, or from one colour to another, such as yellow to green, the table has a subtle difference. From pink to maroon would take three tones, pink (1), deep pink (2), maroon (3). Two or three rows are needed for each change of colour, using the three strands of thread as before.

Fig. 27

35

Modern interpretation of Venetian point lace worked by Daphne Keen using DMC 150 and Coats 60 thread.

BUTTONHOLE STITCHES			CORDING		
Pink	Deep Pink	Maroon	Pink	Deep Pink	Maroon
3	0	0	3	0	0
2	1	0	3	0	0
1	2	0	2	1	0
	3	0	1	2	0
	2	1		3	0
	1	2		2	1
		3		1	2
		3			3

When working trees the lightest colour will be across the top and down one side, leaving the other side in the shade. Work the top-most stitches into the material, then take the thread over the material to the position of the next branch down. Work the first few stitches of the return row into the laid thread and then into the foundation stitches of the foundation row at the top. Place a pin in the material as if working a picot, take the thread around the pin and back to the position of the next branch. Work half-way down the tree in this way.

Change to the next shade of green, work the first few stitches into the top row, work across to the pin, take the needle up through the loop formed by the pin and work back. At the end of the row take the thread across the material to the outside top branch of the opposite side of the tree. Work two or three rows right across with this second colour then continue to work down the three on the first side only. Pin the thread at the end of each row ready to be picked up by the third colour. Remove the pins as each row is worked. Keep the shape of the tree by laying the thread over the material to an outside branch and working back over the laid thread. Further colour changes can be made by working into the stitches already made, linking one area to another by taking a thread across and working back over the laid thread independently of the stitches below.

To work a free-standing tree, use the covered wire (see list of suppliers), bind a number of wires together leaving one leader wire free, and bend the top of each wire into position to form the shape of a tree. Each branch is worked separately then linked together, using colour to give light and shade in the same way as for the embroidery. Once the wires are bound securely and bent to

A design modified from a Honiton lace pricking worked by Pat Gibson, using Anchor stranded embroidery thread.

Pitstone Windmill, Ivinghoe, Dunstable. An original work in needlepoint lace by Mary Kingston $17\frac{1}{4} \times 15$ in $(44 \times 39$ cm$)$. Shades of green wool for working the foliage using pea stitch variation, while the windmill itself is worked in 20 crochet cotton. The sails were worked in beige polyester sewing thread and the bars in black 20 crochet cotton to give a 3-D effect.

A scene worked by Mary Anderson following the directions for the free-standing tree given in this book. The mountain scene and chalet all worked in various needlepoint lace stitches given here using 130/5 silk thread.

shape, turn the very end of each branch over to form a very small loop. Knot the thread to the end of each branch and work around the loop formed, in close buttonhole stitch. Then work along the wire in spaced buttonhole stitch. Work back along this row in uneven groups of stitches; into each space on the return row work a Belle Point de Venise. Leave the thread hanging at the end of the row where the wires are bound together ready to use for the trunk of the tree. Work the branches in three or four different shades of green. When all the branches have been worked they can be linked together working from one branch down to another toward the centre of the tree; leave the outside ends of the branches free to drop down slightly in a natural shape.

The trunk is worked by taking one of the threads left from the branches and the leader wire that was left unbound and working down this wire

in spaced buttonhole stitch sewing to the rest of the wire to about 2 inches (5 cm) from the bottom. Using a thread from the branches and three strands of a grey/brown work around the trunk from the branches down to the base of the trunk to the unbound part of the wires. Don't attempt to work back up the trunk. Rethread the needle at the top each time and work down. Whatever thread is left at the bottom can be used to wrap the roots. The uncovered wires at the bottom form the roots; these are taken in groups and wrapped, then buttonholed over. Bend and buckle the wire to shape, and work groups of stitches to give a gnarled impression. Moss green can be used to give the effect of creeper or lichens.

TAPE LACE
Mixed lace first appeared in the seventeenth century and the Venetian Guipure was called *Mezzo Punto*. This type of lace was also known as *Milan au lacet* and Genoese Guipure. The Venetian Guipure had the same designs, fillings and raised work as Gros Point, but instead of being worked over a cordonnet, a bobbin-made braid was used

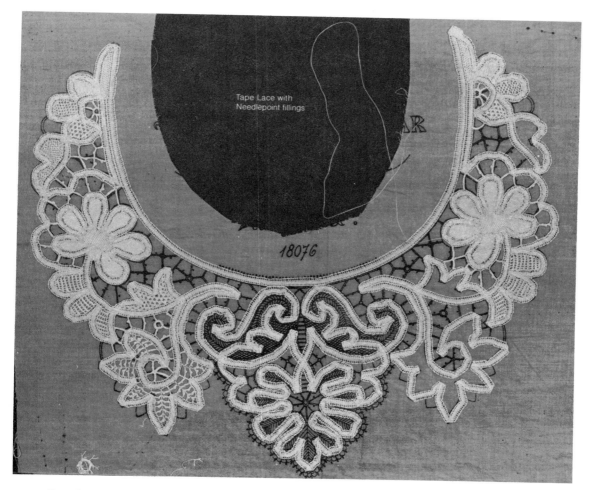

Tape Lace with
Needlepoint fillings

18076

A collar design partially worked, showing the use of
tape and needlepoint stitch fillings.

to outline the design. Both silk and linen thread
were used in the making of these early laces. The
braid was also worked to a design, in the same way
as Bruges or Honiton lace is worked, so that the
curves and corners lie flat and are not gathered.
By the middle of the nineteenth century, hand-
made braids had been replaced by machine-made
tapes, although pedlars still made and sold a
variety of narrow hand-made braids.

By the middle of the nineteenth century tape
lace work had a new impetus; printed glazed cloth
patterns were sold that needed very little in the
way of fillings. It was enough if the worker could
do no more than the spider webb woven wheel
and woven bars. It was at this point that tape lace
found an all-time low. A true lace maker would be
very disdainful of 'tape lace'. Dickle lace was
made entirely of tape, laid to a printed design and

buttonholed over completely, without even a
woven webb to relieve the monotony. Tapes
could be bought in bundles of a dozen yards for a
matter of two or three old pence.

Some tape lace was of a different class. In
England Branscombe Point held first place with a
set number of fillings beautifully executed. In
North America it was the Battenberg lace that
was the most intricate.

Branscombe is a small town in Devon, which
was, and still is, a centre of the needle-made laces
in that part of the country. The name Battenberg
originates from the title 'Countess of Battenberg'
which was bestowed on the Countess of Hauke on
her marriage to Prince Alexander of Hesse in

40

1851. Her third son, Maurice, married the popular Princess Beatrice, fifth daughter of Queen Victoria. It was after this marriage that the tape lace, already widely made in the USA became known as Royal Battenberg lace. Other names for this type of lace at the end of the nineteenth and beginning of this century were Modern Point, Point de Bruges and Ideal Honiton. These last two names are misleading as both Bruges and Honiton are pillow laces, in which the outline is made onto a pricking with bobbin-made fillings. All tape lace should have the outline of the design made this way, as it was back in the seventeenth century, but with needle point fillings.

If tape is to be used, then try to find one made with fine thread and always use a narrow tape, which will remain confined within the double lines of the design. Use a fine needle and minute running stitches for a draw thread. The tape should be folded at a 45° corner, never gathered, and should follow the design as far as possible in an unbroken line. Use as many different fillings as can be accommodated comfortably in one unit of the design, then follow the stitches through in each repeat.

Trace a design, in parallel lines, then cover with acetate film and mount to backing material. Run the draw threads through both edges of the tape for about $\frac{1}{2}$ yard (46 cm) and leave them attached. With a new thread tack the tape to the design, using the draw-threads to gather the tape around the inside of curves, keeping the tape as flat as possible. For the best results, tack both sides of the tape to the design.

A tape lace butterfly.

Tape lace at its lowest ebb.

THE BUTTERFLY COLLECTION

The following designs can be used in many ways. Each design can be worked on its own, in pairs or in groups. They can be mirror imaged to edge collars and cuffs, ends of ties or pockets. Enlarged they fit into the corners of table cloths, reduced and laid in sequence they can be used to edge a bridal veil or be scattered at random over it. They can be used in the same way for a christening gown.

A modern interpretation of the Point de Gaze butterfly found in the Museum of Art and History, Brussels, worked by the author using Knox 220 linen and Hilaturas, Barcelona linen thread.

Fig. 28

Fig. 29

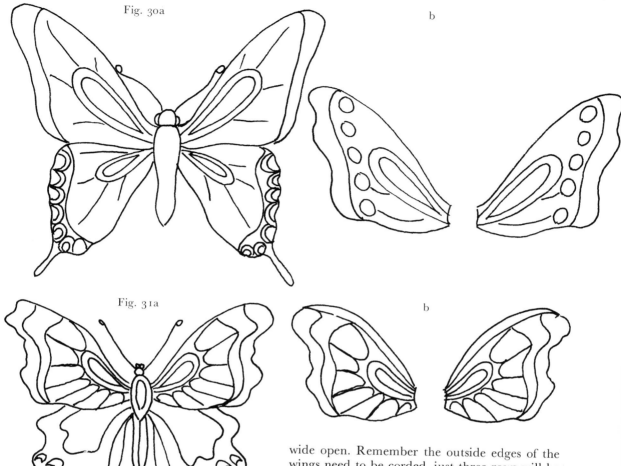

Fig. 30a   b

Fig. 31a   b

Any of these designs will make greetings cards for someone special or for that special occasion such as a twenty-fifth or fiftieth wedding anniversary, worked in either silver or gold lurex thread. Imagine a cream princess-style silk dress with a loose flowing panel covered in two-dimensional butterflies. Or an evening waistcoat in a subtle colour, with butterflies dancing over it, worked in the intense vibrant tones of their wings, all worked in real silk to give the extra depth to the colours. For a bride's head-dress, three white silk creatures could be poised on an Alice band that had been covered in white ribbon with the veil gathered and attached underneath the band.

Ideas for working the stitches have been left

wide open. Remember the outside edges of the wings need to be corded, just three rows will be enough to keep a firm edge. Contrast open stitches with close stitches, the rings can be laid and couched, and any of the wheels can be worked inside the rings, or they can be formed on the ring stick as couronnes and attached afterwards. On any large areas use pea stitch, double Brussels or Ardenza stitch to give some firmness to the lace. Smaller areas can have the more open fillings; do not forget that an open space left in the design, once the cordonnette is laid, gives depth to the work.

Any of these butterflies can be given an extra set of wings by tracing off the top half of each set of the wings only, not the body. The bottom wing need not be as ornate as the top half. When joining the two sets of wings, stitch together along the edge of the body and along the centre of the pair. Try to attach in such a way that the top set appear to be in flight.

Any of the butterfly shapes could be adapted to this square (Fig. 33). The half square was intended to be used for a tray cloth, worked in stranded embroidery cotton, but it has been reduced to fit within the size of the book and in this format it is well proportioned for a wedding handkerchief. So many handkerchief edgings are worked but once finished and mounted they are put away, wrapped in tissue paper. This rather defeats the object; pretty things need to be used, it gives a feeling of luxury that costs so little. A few evenings without television and you have something to use, which the average person could never afford to buy.

Fig. 32a

b

Fig. 33

Point de Gaze butterfly worked by the author using 300 linen thread. The little bee is worked in Alsace thread.

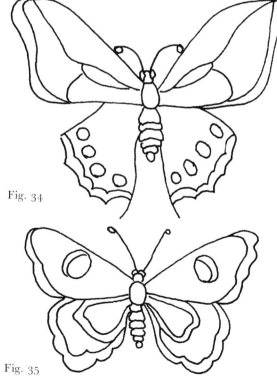

Fig. 34

Fig. 35

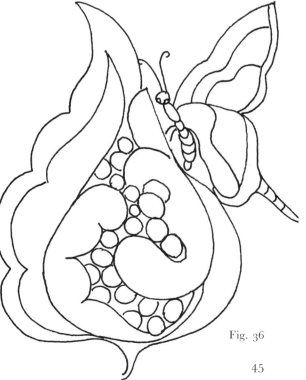

Fig. 36

45

A design worked by Elsa Took in shades of sugar-candy pink silk and applied to the back of a black silk evening jacket.

Worked from the design of a peacock butterfly by Pat Gibson, incorporating horsehair in the cordonette.

Fig. 37

If using any of the other designs, lay the butterfly in each corner first, then bring the floral spray down to fit the shape. A scroll can be used instead of the flower design.

The butterfly on the seed pod could be used on a blouse pocket, on the bodice of a child's dress or maybe two or three could be placed half-way down one side of a skirt. Remember, if worked in stranded embroidery cotton, the design can be lifted off any garment and remounted at a later date onto something else. As long as the threads are joined in and fastened off properly, worked motifs outlast most garments.

The large shapes can be used to fit in a lampshade ring, to hang at a window where the sun can shine through to cast butterfly shadows on the walls. They are big enough to be worked in the heavier silk threads when they look very good placed across the back of a dressing gown or lounger.

47

Fig. 38

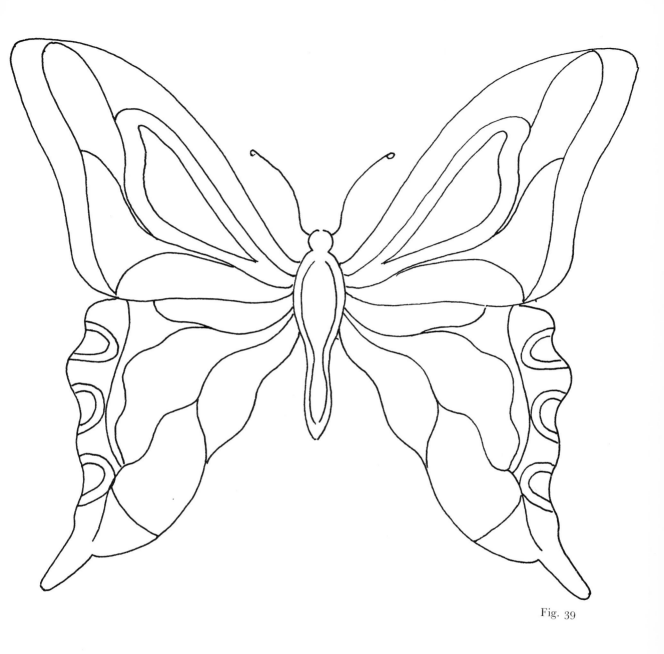

Fig. 39

Fig. 40

Fig. 41

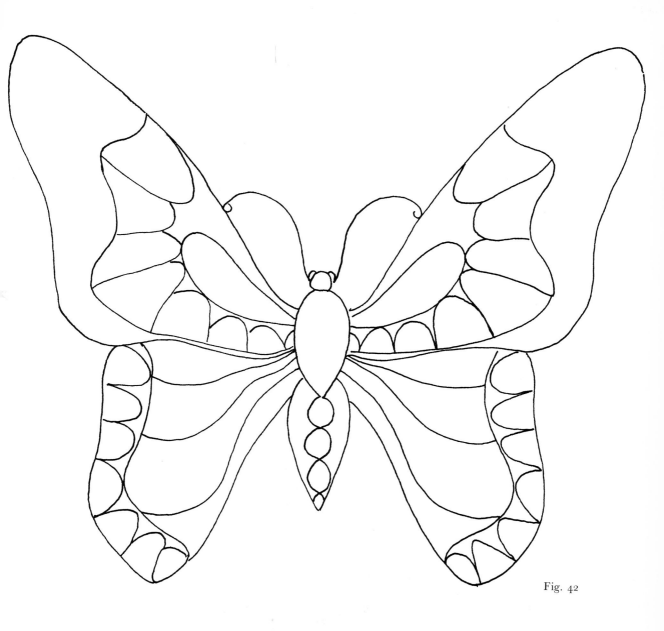

Fig. 42

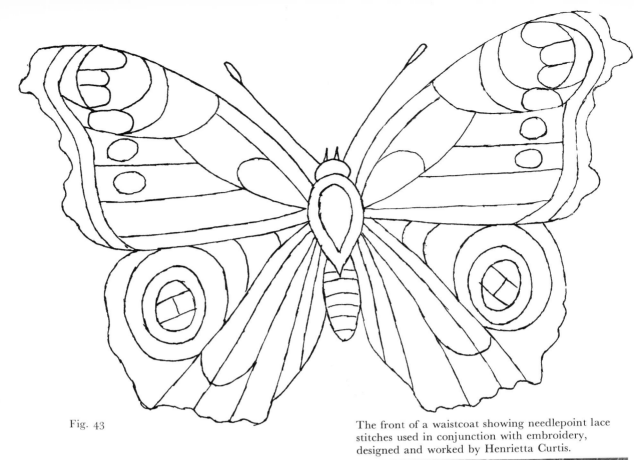

Fig. 43

The front of a waistcoat showing needlepoint lace
stitches used in conjunction with embroidery,
designed and worked by Henrietta Curtis.

LACE BOUQUETS

Free-standing lace flowers are reasonably quick to make because each individual flower is small and worked in straightforward stitches. When three or five flowers are turned into a spray, with two or three leaves added, they make a very acceptable birthday of Christmas gift. By choosing the favourite flower of the recipient, it becomes a very personal gift.

The following selection of petals and leaves make up into charming bouquets for evening wear or they can be fixed into an unusual container for standing on a dressing table or coffee table.

To make the flowers and leaves, first trace off four or five petals of the same shape and couch to the backing in the normal way. Use fine white linen thread, or, if working in colour, use silk thread.

Keep to the minimum of stitches, corded stitch for the leaves, pea stitch, single or double Brussels and Ardenza stitches for the petals.

The finest white millinery wire is needed to lay in with the cordonnette for the larger flowers, while horsehair will be enough for the smaller shapes. Fine florists' wire will be needed for the stalks; this is sometimes covered with green thread, but if it is plain wire it will need to be covered by wrapping, using the same type of thread as is being used for the flowers. Put a minute spot of Copydex on the end of the wire to hold the thread when you start the winding.

Miniature sprays and arrangements need containers in keeping with their size and shape. Bric-a-brac stalls at antique markets often yield unexpected bargains. The little Japanese vase was found for just a few pennies. The spray of canary rose fits perfectly in the bowl of the Chinese spoon. A conch shell with a pale pink mother-of-pearl interior would look lovely with dog roses. The china eggs that are so popular make ideal containers, the two halves can be held apart with fine

A collection of miniature pots, featuring a Dartington glass violet bowl, a Wedgwood pot, and three items found for a few pence on antique stalls.

Selection of four ceramic pots made by Yvonne
Dowell and one miniature silver violet bowl made
by Neil Lovesey.

white card, cut and bent to shape and held in
place with white masking tape. Lace flowers are
then arranged to fall over the side and fill the
opening between the two halves. It is always
possible to pick up the odd minute coffee cup and
saucer. A china tea pot from a doll's tea set can be
used with effect.

Getting down to everyday objects, there are the
small honey pots that come in sets of six in gift
boxes. Around Christmas time, mustard is often
sold in little Delft pots; these often have the added
bonus of a basket-work handle. Slightly larger
pots can be found full of crystallized ginger. There
are the china pots that hold 'Gentleman's Relish',
which are about 3 inches (75 mm) in diameter.

These are just a few ideas, but once the
imagination has been caught the most remark-
able things will turn up.

CONVOLVULUS

Work the whole spray in corded stitch, either

130/3 silk or one strand taken from DMC or
Anchor stranded embroidery cotton.

The convolvulus flower is made up of five
petals. When first starting to open they appear to
have the very palest tint of yellow/green at the
base of the trumpet, but are pure white when fully
opened. The calyx which forms a cup around the
base of the trumpet is made up of two bracts. The
outside edge is the colour of seaweed while the
centre of each bract is yellow/green.

Buds are cream, sometimes lemon-yellow, with
a calyx the same size, shape and colour as the one
at the base of the flower.

The leaves are spear shaped, mid-green in
colour with lighter green veining and stand at
right angles to the stalks. The stalks and tendrils
all twist clockwise around whatever they are
climbing up and some tendrils just twist in mid-
air.

Trace the shape of the petal off five times for the
flower and two extra to form the bud (Fig. 44).
The calyx will need to be traced off, fitting the
bracts into spaces left between the petals. Prepare
onto backing material and couch, using the same
colour thread as the petals. Work the five flower

54

Fig. 44

petals in corded stitch, starting at the base of the trumpet and working to the top. To allow for the extra width across the top of the petal it will be necessary to work half rows in the following manner:

Take the corded thread from the base to the top of the petal and buttonhole half-way down the length, return the corded thread back to the top of the petal and work a quarter of the way down. Lay the corded thread back to the top of the petal and work down to the base. To avoid a hole appearing at the two points where the corded thread was returned, take the nearest buttonhole stitch before the return and take the needle through this stitch and behind the corded thread, then continue in the usual way, working cording stitch down to the next break in the line at the half-way mark. Do the same thing again, take the needle through the nearest stitch behind the corded thread, then continue to the end of the row. Work two straight rows from top to bottom, then reverse the procedure. Work a quarter of the way down, then cord back, then half-way down and cord back, then the complete rows again. Continue until the stitching has filled the top of the petal. Work all five petals and four bracts, lay the cordonnette around the bracts starting from the base of each one using at least four threads and adding another two as the work proceeds over the top of the bract, cut out two threads half-way

down to the other side. Knot the working thread into the first stitch, then leave the threads from the cordonnette and the working thread hanging. Next lay the cordonnette down both sides of each petal, not across the top, and again leave the threads hanging from the base of each petal as this is used to anchor the finished flower to the wire stalk. Remove the petals from the backing material, pull all loose couch stitches away and re-lay the petal just touching its neighbour. Now lay and work a cordonnette around all five tops, joining them into the circle. Remove from backing and join each petal to its neighbour to form a trumpet.

Take a wire for the stalk and fold over the end for about $\frac{1}{2}$ inch (12 mm) to form the pistil, join a strand of pink thread to the fold and bind tightly around the wire up to the top of the fold. Take the thread through the hole formed at the bend in the wire, then buttonhole over the bound wire for the length of the fold. Change to a pale green thread and continue to buttonhole over the wire for about 1 inch (24 mm), carefully fasten off. The wire is taken through the trumpet and all threads hanging from the petals are twisted tightly around the wire at the base of the flower. Fasten off by stab stitching through the twisted threads a number of times in four different directions, then

55

stitch the threads to the base of the trumpet and fasten off.

Remove the finished bracts from the backing material, clean off the couch stitches that may be still in the cordonnette, sew the two together to form a cup, one bract slightly overlapping the other, then push the stalk through the base and take the calyx up to the base of the flower, stitch into place through the threads wrapped around the wire, then through the base of each petal.

The bud petals are worked in the same way as the flower petals. Lay the cordonette all around and leave the threads hanging. Remove from

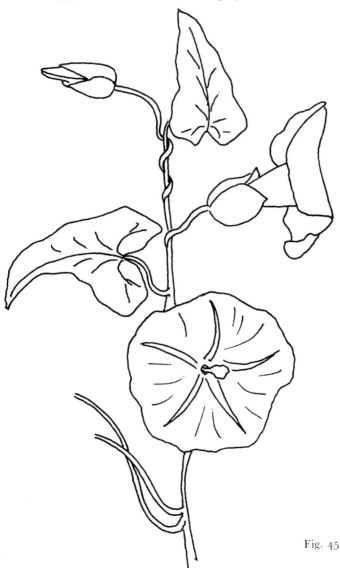

Fig. 45

backing material, clean off the couch stitch ends. Take one petal, stitch the long sides together, to form a cone. Bend the end of a wire over and roll a small quantity of cotton wool around the end and insert into the centre of the cone, then stitch around the base of the petal and draw up tightly to hold the wire secure. The point of the second petal is stitched to the base and folded around the first petal to form the bud. Fix the calyx in the same way as given for the flower.

The leaves can be shaded from one side through to the other or worked from the base up to the tip, depending on where the colour needs to change. Follow the instructions given in chapter 3 in the section on colour for changing from one tone of colour to another, substituting light, medium and a deeper green for the pinks given. Lay the cordonnette and work with the medium green and again leave the threads hanging, to fix the leaf to the stalk. Lay the tip of the leaf to the end of a wire and stitch down the centre of the leaf, by bringing the working thread up through the leaf over just one stitch and back through the leaf. Take the working thread over the wire and back up through the leaf. When joining any part of a flower or leaf etc. together, take up just one stitch at a time in this way, and the joins will be hard to detect.

Remember to twist one stalk around another clockwise and the tendrils are twisted around a size $2\frac{3}{4}$ (12 old size) knitting needle, always clockwise.

THE POPPY

This is a little more complicated to work than the convolvulus, but well worth the extra trouble. Draw up the four petals and two sections of the calyx and prepare onto backing materials (Fig. 46). Each petal has a black laid thread at the base, couched down with black thread. The rest of the petal is laid and couched in red. The poppy shown on pages 59 and 60 was worked in 130/3 silk throughout. Take the black thread, fold in half and start at the edge where the dividing line is shown on the petal, work down around the base and up the other side to the dividing line. Take a length of red silk, fold in half and continue to couch up the side of the petal over the top and down to the line where the black started. Take the red laid thread through the loop formed by the fold in the black thread then couch the red thread back on itself until half-way up the side of the

Convolvulus spray designed and worked by the author, showing the front view of the convolvulus.

The back view of the convolvulus. The flowers, leaves and buds are not wired but the stalks are constructed using covered florists' wire.

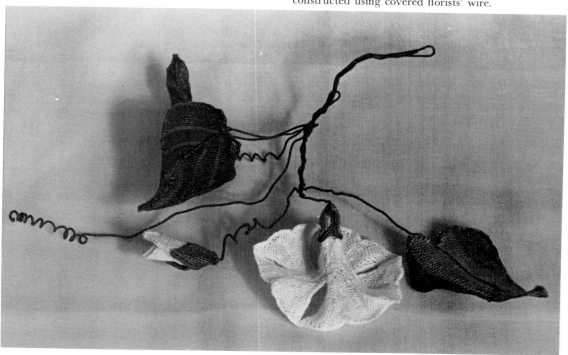

Fig. 46

Front view of a poppy.

petal. Rethread the needle with black thread, take the black thread through the loop formed at the start of the red laid thread, then back down to the base of the petal. If this isn't done the couched threads will separate when the work is removed from the backing. The base of each petal is worked with black in corded stitch, starting with one stitch into the point on the first row then each side of the first stitch on the next row. From then on, increase the stitches on both sides to fill the space until reaching the dividing line.

Change to the darkest red and work along the side of the petal from the top edge down to the black, join by taking the needle under and up through the end stitch of each row as the work progresses across the petal. Shade the red through two or three changes of colour through to the centre of the petal, then back through the same colour changes to the dark red on the other side of the petal. See table on page 35.

As with the convulvulus it will be necessary to work the half rows and quarter rows to fill the extra space across the top of the petal. Having worked the petal, cordonnette the base with six threads of black and the black thread for the buttonhole stitches from one dividing line around the bottom of the base and up to the start of the red, use eight red threads to lay for the cordonnette for the remainder of the petal. Gradually cut the threads out over the last six stitches. Make sure to knot off the red working thread securely.

Rethread the black working thread and make a series of picots $\frac{1}{8}$ inch (3 mm) in length along the dividing line between the red and black, forming them to lay out from the base of the petal over the red to represent the stamens. Finish the other three petals in the same way, remove from backing material and take any couch threads out that still remain.

Take a wire for the stalk; poppies have very slender stalks so use the finest covered wire, bend one end around into a ring, and with black thread work very close buttonhole stitch around the wire to form a hub. Sew the four petals to the back of this hub. The calyx is made up of two green sections which are sewn into position over the base of the petals. The head of the flower is bent at right angles to the stalk and each petal needs to be folded up to give a crumpled effect, then lightly rolled back and put into its final position.

The leaves may look difficult but there is not

very much work in each piece. They do need wiring from the tip down through the centre of the leaf. The rest of the leaf will fall into place if the centre is given a slight curve out from the stalk of the flower when the two stalks are twisted together. The tip of the leaf usually reaches up as high as the bottom petal of the flower leaving both buds and flowers free of any greenery. One half of the petal shape is enough for a bud, which is then sewn into a cone, a wire for the stalk is folded in the same way as instructed for the bud of the convolvulus, wrapped with a little cotton wool inserted into the cone. The base is drawn together by working rounds of buttonhole stitch to fill the area (see Fig. 48).

Lay the cordonnet around the outer edge of the oval and join the working thread at A. Work two

Back view of a poppy. Also designed and worked by the author in the same manner as the convolvulus.

Fig. 47

A

Fig. 48

rows of spaced buttonhole stitch. Whip the base of
each loop, keeping the filling flat. Work over the
whipped loops for one row. Whip the base of each
loop as in the third row. Repeat rows 4 and 3 as
many times as needed to fill the space.

Make the two sections of the calyx for the bud,
join together at the base around the stalk, pinch
the bud between finger and thumb to flatten
slightly. Take both sections of the calyx to the top
of the bud and sew together for about $\frac{1}{4}$ inch
(6 mm), leaving the two sides open and allowing
the red of the bud to show through. Bend the wire
to allow the bud to hang down and give the stalk
one or two bends because the heads really are too
heavy for the stalks.

A honey-coloured straw hat with the poppy and
convolvulus flowers arranged in a Hogarth curve.

THE VIOLET

This needs patience to put together but as everything about it is so tiny it takes no more time than some of the other flowers given.

The leaves are straightforward, being shaded through a range of three or four shades of green, either from the tip down to the stalk or from one side to the other. Lay a cordonnette of four threads, adding two extra around the base both sides of the stalk. The veining is rows of cordonnette worked over the finished leaf. The stalk starts at the tip of the leaf and bends away from the flower. The flower has five petals, the bottom one is slightly larger than the other four (Fig. 49). The colour change is not so much through a petal as each one varies from its neighbour. The top two stand upright and are darker than the other three that hang slightly away from the top two. Each little petal has a white patch at the base.

Small ramekin pot filled with violets worked in 130/3 silks, by the author.

The calyx is made up of six spikes and can be worked as one whole.

The wire for the stalk needs to be bent over at the very edge and bound with yellow thread. The five petals can be sewn to the calyx and then are pushed through and secured at the back. The stalk comes straight up behind the two top petals and bends away in a curve. Under the stalk is a little brown seed pod that curves up and is attached to the completed flower when everything else is sewn together. These flowers were all worked in 130/3 silk; neither the petals nor leaves need any form of stiffening apart from the addition of the wire stalk.

Captured driftwood, completely taken over by dog roses, honeysuckle and ivy. Made by Doreen Holmes using a single strand of Anchor stranded embroidery cotton.

Fig. 49

64

AUSTRIAN BRIAR

Austrian briar is known here as the canary bird weeping rose tree.

The flowers are of a bright yellow and the stalks are a fresh spring green. There are five petals to each flower, but each one is separate at the base. Make the stamens in the same way as those for the dog rose and attach them in the same way.

Make each petal as in Fig. 50; the buds are worked in the round.

Fig. 50

WILD CYCLAMEN

The flowers each have five petals which are joined at the base to form a ring. The bottom of this ring is then turned in to form a trumpet, the petals folding upwards. The stalk is fixed in this trumpet and comes out at the side of the flower as shown in Fig. 51. The buds are made up of five petals, each needing only three rows of corded stitch. Use the very finest wire to edge just one side of each petal. Insert the stalk, lay the petals around it, and work the calyx in the round. When all the petals are fixed, carefully twist the whole bud anti-clockwise as in the diagram.

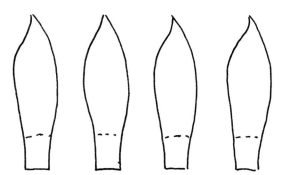

Fig. 51

65

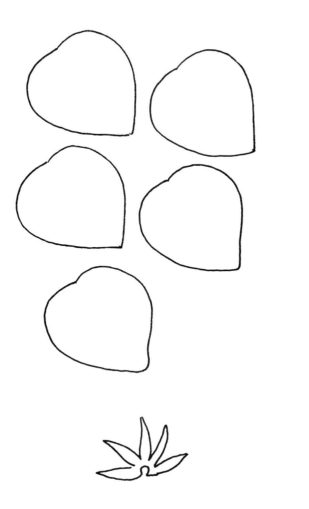

THE CRANESBILL

The cranesbill has five petals and needs only five small rings to form the stamens. Two flowers are joined by a forked stem, then down into the main stem. The flowers are a lavender-blue, and the leaves are a sage-green. Work the two shapes given for the leaves and one should overlap the other.

Fig. 52

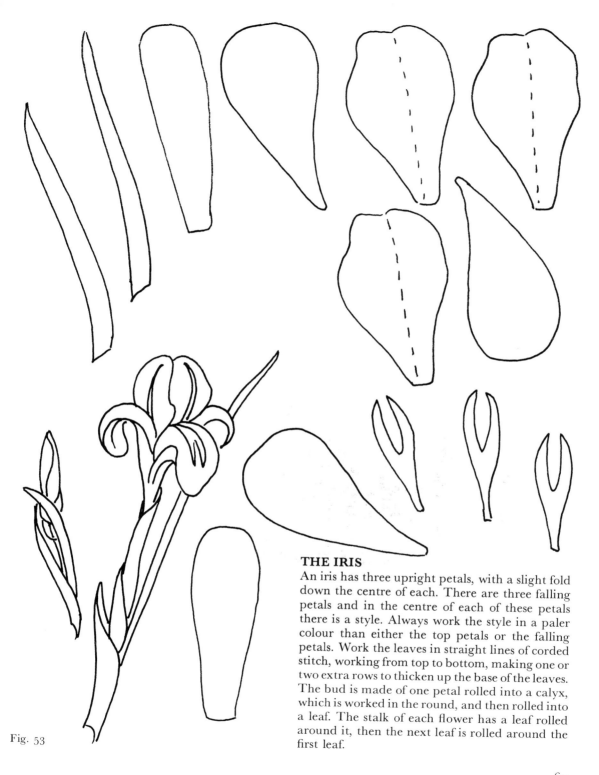

THE IRIS
An iris has three upright petals, with a slight fold down the centre of each. There are three falling petals and in the centre of each of these petals there is a style. Always work the style in a paler colour than either the top petals or the falling petals. Work the leaves in straight lines of corded stitch, working from top to bottom, making one or two extra rows to thicken up the base of the leaves. The bud is made of one petal rolled into a calyx, which is worked in the round, and then rolled into a leaf. The stalk of each flower has a leaf rolled around it, then the next leaf is rolled around the first leaf.

Fig. 53

67

Pansy designed and worked by Pat Gibson in shades
of yellow and deep purple in corded Brussels stitch,
using 100/3 silks.

POINT DE GAZE FLOWERS

This lace has many differently shaped flowers but those with the applied petals are all worked in the same way, only the centres differ. The base petals are worked half-way down in corded stitch and then the other half is worked in Brussels stitch.

All the applied petals are worked in corded stitch, the only variation being where the four little holes forming the diamonds are placed.

The centres are made up of a variety of ring stick or woven wheels, Alençon beads and rows of Point d'Angleterre roses woven from one side to the other.

The separate petals and the base flower have the cordonnette worked before being assembled. The applied petals are placed at different angles in two or three layers on top of the finished base flower. The same design can be used for a number of flowers, changing the appearance by positioning the applied petals differently.

WORKING THE FOUR-HOLE DIAMOND

The diamond is usually found worked in conjunction with the corded stitch as it is more prominent in this stitch than in any other. Miss the corded thread as well as the loops, except at the bottom hole; in this case work over three threads (two corded threads and the previous loop).

1st row Work across the row to where the first loop is to be placed, miss a loop and continue to work across the row.

2nd row Work across to the loop prior to the hole left in the previous row, miss this loop, work two stitches into the hole above, miss a loop then continue the row.

3rd row Work two stitches into the hole left in row 2 and leave a loop directly under the loop missed on the first row, then work two stitches into the next hole left in row 2.

4th row Make two stitches over the three threads into the hole left in row 3.

FLOWER NO. 1 (Fig. 56)

Trace off the base flower and the three separate petals, cover with acetate film and tack to backing material. Couch around the outside edge of base flower and the top and bottom lines that hold the two sets of wheels.

Follow the diagram to place the foundation for the first half of the top row of rings and couch in position. Then lay the other foundation row.

Work the top of each petal down to the first couched thread in corded stitch. Next to be worked is the top row of rings, with the knot of the buttonhole stitch always to the outside. Work the first foundation thread, turning the work at each curve to the most comfortable position. Work

V-front and boned collar for an Edwardian blouse in white cotton voile, designed and worked by Catherine Barley using 120 industrial sewing cotton.

Fig. 56

Antique lace showing the four hole diamond
described on page 69.

back along the second foundation thread and at the point where the two threads cross, take the needle under and up through the loop of the previous row, before continuing along the next part of the curve. This keeps the rings lying flat.

The space between the two sets of rings is worked in Brussels stitch, using the bottom couched thread of the rings just worked for the foundation row. Anchor to the top couched line of the second set of wheels. Work seven or eight ring stick wheels and join to top and bottom of the couched line and to each other by taking the thread through the stitches of the wheels. It may be necessary to use a finer needle to do this.

Make one large ring stick wheel for the hub and lay in position, then work five Alençon bars between the hub and the lowest couched thread of the second set of wheels.

The three separate petals are next worked in corded stitch placing the little diamonds in position. With such a pronounced division in the petals it is best to start at the right-hand top corner and work down the petal to the centre curve, then start again at the top left-hand corner and work down to the centre curve, working across the rows to finish the petal. The last petal can be turned upside down and worked from the bottom, increasing on each row as the petal becomes wider.

Work the cordonnette around the base flower and the separate petals and remove from the backing material. Always cut the threads between the layers of backing material to remove the lace to avoid cutting the stitches of the lace. Pull all the little threads of the couching from behind the lace carefully. If any threads have been split by the working thread, carefully shear off as close as possible. Then apply the three petals in the position shown in the diagram.

Fig. 55

Collar designed by Catherine Barley, for her blouse. (Not to scale.)

Fig. 54

Bodice front, designed by Catherine Barley, for her
blouse. (Not to scale.)

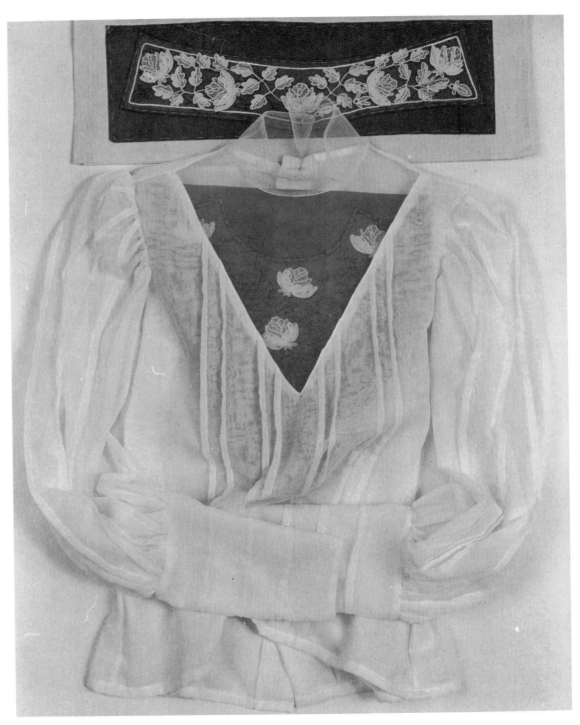

The unfinished lace is shown in position to give a
general effect.

FLOWER NO. 2

Trace off and prepare in the same way as given for the first flower. The petals of the main flower can be worked as a sampler, working a different stitch into each petal or using just three stitches in turn.

Make a ring stick hub for the centre and tack into position. Then work six or seven smaller rings for the top band, stitch the top and bottom cordonnets above the hub. Connect the hub and the rings with Ardenza bars then work the cordonnette along the top and bottom couched threads.

When laying the cordonnette around the flower petals, take the four threads up to a curve at the tip of each petal, leave two threads and take the other two across the top line and work back. Pick up the other two threads and work the curve to form a continuous line around the outside edge of the petal.

The four separate petals are worked in corded stitch with or without the four-hole diamonds.

Once the cordonnette is worked, remove from the backing material, pull all the cut ends from the back of the lace, then sew the loose petals into position.

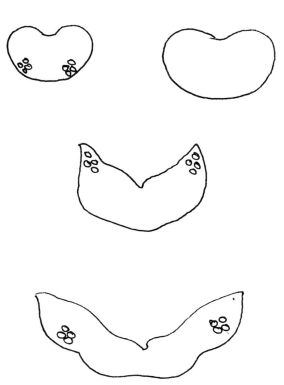

Fig. 57

75

Fig. 58

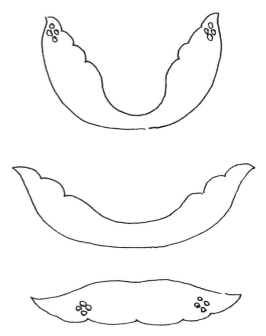

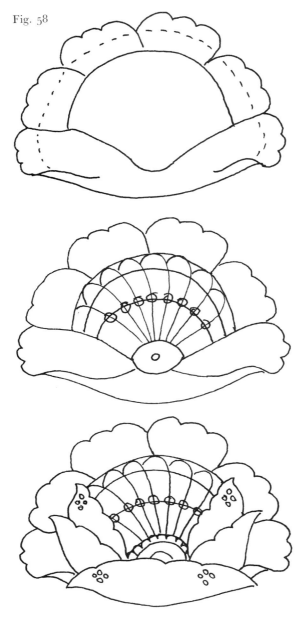

FLOWER NO. 3

Lay the cordonnet around the base flower, work the petals to the dotted line in corded stitch and finish to the base of each petal in Brussels stitch. Work a ring stick wheel with scallops for the hub and tack in place. Lay and couch the two curved lines and work the top curve in buttonhole stitch. Next take a thread from the hub to the first couched line and make a knot stitch, take the thread through a buttonhole stitch on the top curved line and up to the base of the first top petal. Return, taking the thread under and over the cordonnet, back through a buttonhole stitch down to the couched thread and make a knot stitch, then through the back of a hub stitch. Retrace along the same line taking the needle through the last knot stitch formed, so holding the two threads together, on through the same buttonhole stitch on the next line up, then to the base of a petal. Lay nine or ten loops in this way.

Starting on one side at the top, work over the curve under the petal in buttonhole stitch, down to the first couched thread, take the needle behind the buttonhole stitches on this thread and down to the hub, taking the thread through the back of a hub stitch. Buttonhole back up over the next laid threads to the top couched thread, take the thread through the last loop of the buttonhole stitches that have formed the first curve, then work back over the curve. Repeat, working each section in the same way.

Work a small wheel at the intersection of each set of threads on the lower couched thread. Work the cordonnette along the lines shown in the diagram. Lay the cordonnet and work the three loose petals in corded stitch, then work the cordonnettes before removing from the backing material. Remove all cut ends before making up.

FLOWER NO. 4

Couch the base flower, the stalk and the two loose petals. Work down to the dotted line in corded stitch, then work the remainder of each petal in Brussels stitch.

Next lay a cordonnet around the centre piece and lay and couch the three curved rows. Work nine or ten ring stick wheels and sew into position slightly overlapping the top cordonnet.

Take a thread from the hub up to the first wheel, knotting on passing the couched threads, then whip back to the hub. Pass the needle through two or three stitches at the back of the hub and back up to the next wheel, knotting at each couched thread as before. Continue to lay a thread to each wheel and whipping back to the hub.

Starting on one side of the bottom couched thread, form a row of Point d'Angleterre.

Whip up to the next couched thread and work a row of buttonhole stitches with a picot placed centrally to each section.

Whip to the top couched thread and work another row of Point d'Angleterre, slightly larger than the first row.

Work the two loose petals in corded stitch and work the cordonnettes, The left and right bottom petals have the cordonnette worked along the straight edges before laying around the curve of the petals. Continue to lay the cordonnette around the remaining petals.

Remove from the backing material, pull out all the ends of the couching stitches, sew the centre in position, leaving the top wheels overlapping the base of the top petals, then sew the loose petals over the base of the centrepiece.

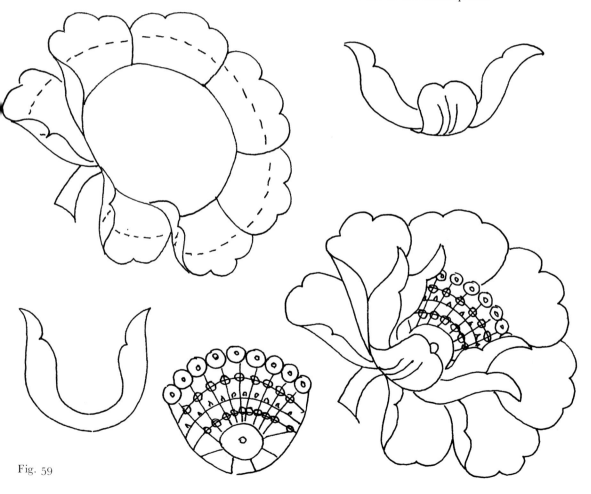

Fig. 59

Flower no. 4 designed and worked by the author,
using 130/3 and 200/3 silk threads in shades of pink
and aubergine.

FLOWER NO. 5

Couch the base flower, the stalk and the three loose petals. Work the top portion of the three top petals in corded stitch. The bottom areas of the two lower petals are also corded.

Work down to the first line of the top petal and the remainder of the other four petals in Brussels stitch.

Work the three loose petals in corded stitch, making the four-hole diamond each side of the top petal.

Lay and work the cordonnette around the base flower and the loose petals. Lay the cordonnet for the centre. Work a ring stick wheel for the hub and eight or nine smaller wheels. Sew the smaller wheels into position, slightly overlapping the top cordonnette and sew the hub into place.

Use four threads for the bottom band, couch into position, and work an Ardenza bar the complete width. Working from the hub to the Ardenza bar, make three or four Alençon beads.

Starting from the Ardenza bar, take a thread up to a ring and whip back to the bar. Whip along the loops of the bar and take the thread up to the next ring and whip back. Continue to join the rest of the rings in the same way. From one side, take a thread across to the first upright thread, make a knot stitch, then across to the next thread, knot and continue over the remaining threads. Then form a row of Point d'Angleterre at each intersection between the Ardenza bar and the top wheels.

Remove from the backing, sew the centre to the base flower and attach the three loose petals.

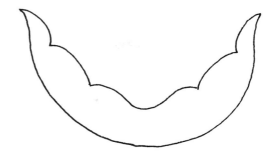

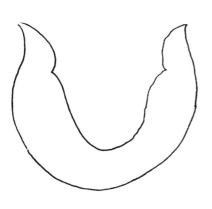

Fig. 60

FLOWER NO. 6

This is not a Point de Gaze flower, the shape was taken from a Jacobean design. The base petals have been used as a sampler, the applied petals were corded and the centre made up of wheels worked on a ring stick.

The petals have been numbered to make direction for applying them easier. Numbers 2 and 4 are sewn in at the base and left while petal no. 3 is sewn into position. 1 and 5 are then sewn in place and 2 and 4 are lifted up and over 1, 3 and 5 then sewn down over the rings and into the base flower.

The rings within the seed pod can all be worked over a ring stick or over nos. 12, 11, 10 and 8 knitting needles.

The rings are joined together by threading the needle with the end of the thread of one ring, take the thread up through an edge stitch of its neighbouring ring and run around the ring under the buttonhole stitches twice. It is only possible to pass the needle through four or five stitches of the ring at a time so always work from the back of the rings. Each ring is joined to its neighbour or to the edge of the design by the end of its working thread; so, when finishing a ring, don't cut off its end.

Fig. 61

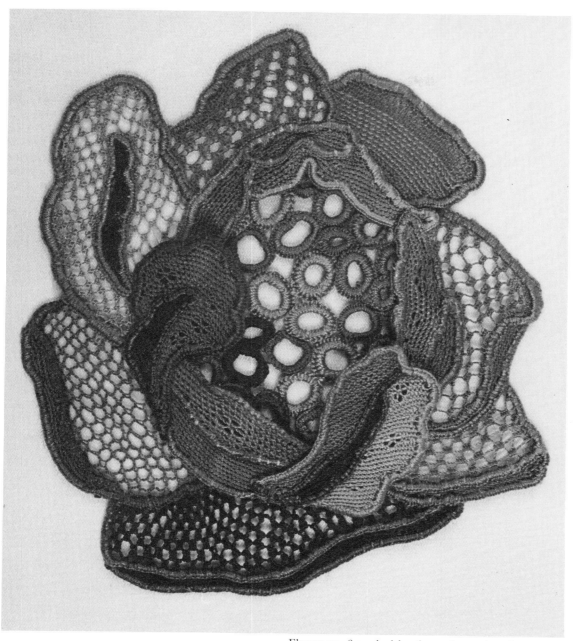

Flower no. 6 worked by the author, taken from a
Jacobean design. Worked in 130/3 and 200/3 silk
thread in shades of seaweed greens.

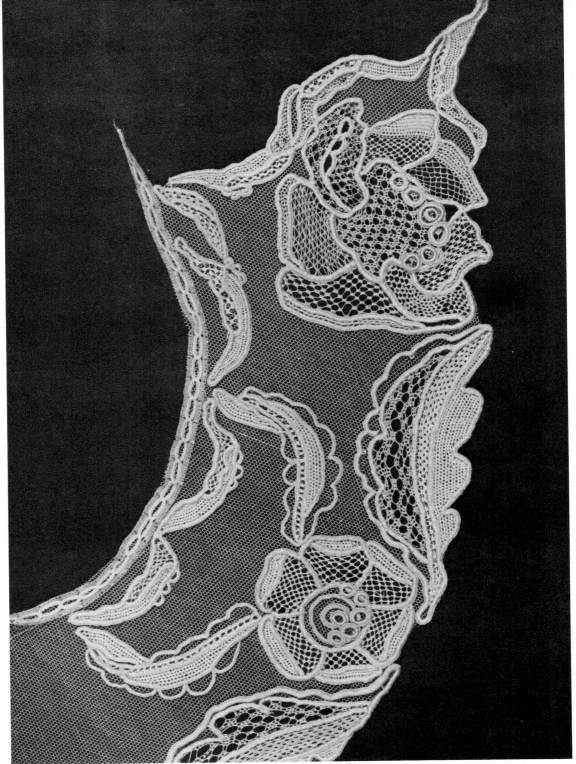

Part of a collar designed and worked by Ann Forbes-Cockell with 80, 100, and 150 crochet cottons using the Point de Gaze flowers given in this chapter.

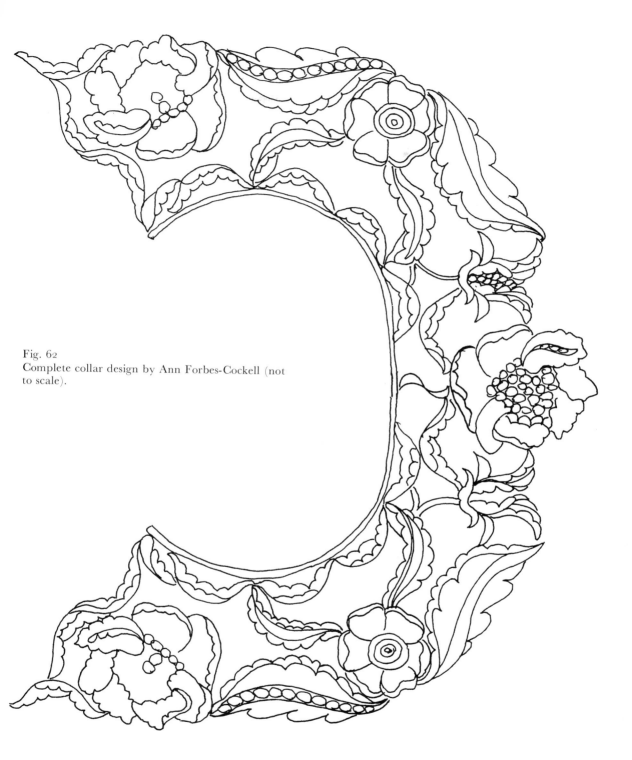

Fig. 62
Complete collar design by Ann Forbes-Cockell (not to scale).

STITCHES

FILLING NO. 1

Work a foundation row of close buttonhole stitches.

1st row   Make a stitch into each loop of the previous row.

2nd row   Work one buttonhole stitch into the first two loops, miss five loops and repeat across the row.

3rd row   Work two stitches into each long loop, miss the small loop and repeat.

4th row   Work six stitches into each long loop and one stitch into the short loops.

5th and 6th rows   Work one stitch into every loop to form a band of close stitches. Repeat the pattern from row 2; check that the number of stitches remains the same on every second and fifth rows over the same width, excluding such increases as will be necessary when working around a curve.

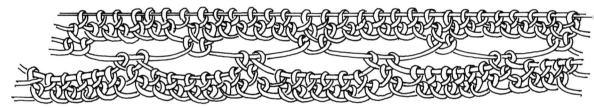

Fig. 63

FILLING NO. 2

Work the foundation row of spaced buttonhole stitches, each loop long enough to accommodate five stitches. It is difficult to give actual lengths for stitches, because of the different size threads being used for each project.

1st row   Into each loop of the foundation row, work five buttonhole stitches.

2nd row   Take the needle under and out through the loop between the first and second set of five stitches. Whip under and over the loop just made twice. Proceed to the loop between the next set of stitches and repeat.

These two rows form the pattern.

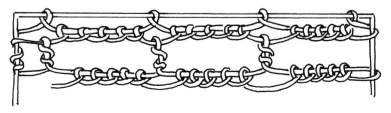

Fig. 64

84

BELLE AND RÉSEAU

Commence by working two rows of buttonhole stitches.

3rd row Make a stitch into the first loop, *miss five loops and make a stitch into the sixth loop. Continue across the space from *.

4th row Into each long loop work seven buttonhole stitches.

5th row Work one stitch into the loop between each group of seven stitches of the previous row.

6th row Into each loop work five stitches.

7th row Work one stitch into each loop of the five stitches on the previous row, giving groups of four.

8th row Work one stitch into each loop as before, giving groups of three stitches.

9th row Work one stitch in the centre of each long loop.

10th row Work a row of buttonhole stitches using seven stitches to fill each long loop of row 9.

The pattern starts again at row 5.

Fig. 65

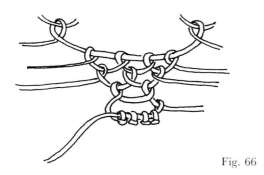

Fig. 66

TREBLE BRUSSELS STITCH

Over the cordonnet work groups of three stitches leaving a loop between each group corresponding to the width of the three stitches.

*Take the working thread around the cordonnet at the side of the space and back again across the row lying level with the bottom of the loops. On the next row work three stitches into the loops between the groups of three of the previous row, taking the needle behind the laid thread as well as the loop making the buttonhole stitch over two threads each time. Repeat from *.

BELLE TOILE

Work the foundation row of buttonhole stitches across the space being filled, then into the loops work another two rows of buttonhole stitches.

4th row Work one buttonhole stitch into every fifth loop.

5th, 6th, 7th and 8th rows Make a Belle Point de Venise into each loop. See page 76 of *The Technique of Needlepoint Lace*, or follow the diagram below.

9th row Make one stitch into the loop between each bell.

10th row Work five stitches into each loop of row 9.

11th row Work into each loop of the stitches on the previous row.

12th row Work another row of buttonhole stitches into loops of row 11. There should be the same number of stitches on this row as there was on the foundation row.

The pattern starts again from row 4.

Fig. 67

85

CINQ POINT GROUND

Work the first, second and third rows of Belle Point de Venise Cinq Point. Then continue as follows:

4th row　Into each loop work two buttonhole stitches.

5th row　Work one buttonhole stitch into the loops between the two stitches of the previous row. At the end of each fifth row, check that there are the same number of loops as were in the third row over the same distance. Stitches can be added or omitted as the pattern demands.

6th row　Work as second row of Cinq Point filling, to give another row of Belle Point.

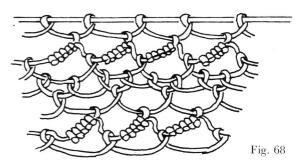

Fig. 68

VARIATIONS ON BELLE POINT DE VENISE CINQ POINT

Commence at the right side and work a row of buttonhole stitches evenly spaced.

2nd row　Work a buttonhole stitch into the first space of the preceding row, then into the loop just formed work five buttonhole stitches close together.

Make sure to draw the first stitch well back. Continue in this way into each loop across the space being filled.

3rd row　Work a buttonhole stitch between each bell.

These two rows form the pattern. Work a sample square before attempting to fill an area in a piece of lace, because it takes a while to get the tension right. Each little 'bell' should be the same size as its neighbour.

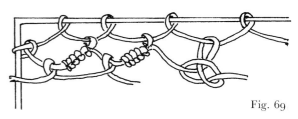

Fig. 69

POINT BRABAÇON

Work the foundation row of buttonhole stitches.

1st row　*Work one stitch into each of the first two loops, miss the next seven loops, then work one stitch into the next two loops, miss two loops, work the next two loops, miss seven and repeat from *.

2nd row　Work seven stitches into the long loops and two stitches in the short loops between the sets of two stitches.

3rd row　Work two buttonhole stitches each side of the two stitches on the short loop of the previous row. Miss the group of seven stitches and repeat.

Repeat the last two rows to form the pattern.

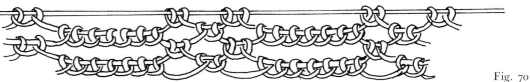

Fig. 70

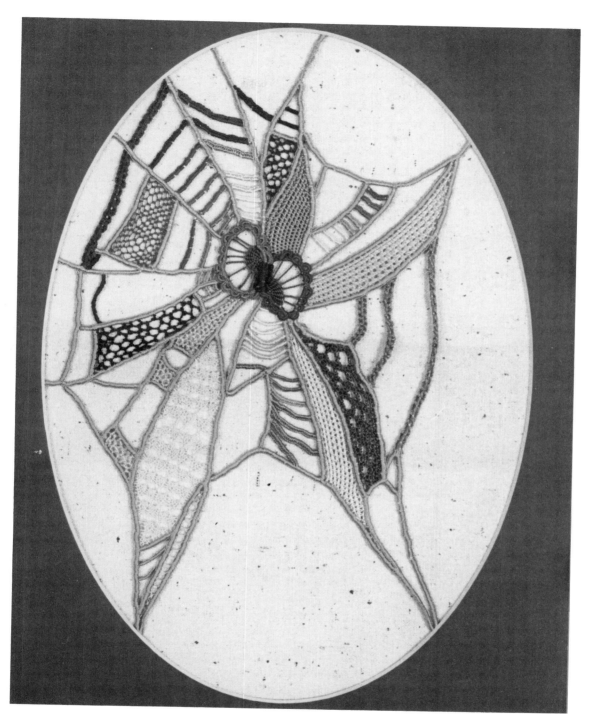

A cobweb worked by Ann Forbes-Cockell using
coloured silks of differing weights and shades of
honey gold through to maroon, illustrating stitches
found in this book and my previous one.

A BURANO FILLING

Lay the foundation row of spaced buttonhole stitches along the length of the ground.

1st row Work two buttonhole stitches into each of the first two loops, miss three loops and repeat.

2nd row Work five buttonhole stitches into the long loops of row 1.

3rd row Work a buttonhole stitch into each loop of the five stitches of row 2.

4th row Work four buttonhole stitches over the two long loops of the previous rows.

5th row Work five stitches into the long loops of row 4.

6th row Work a stitch into each of the five loops of row 5.

Rows 4, 5 and 6 form the pattern.

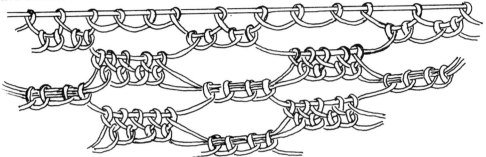

Fig. 71

From a piece of antique lace known as Kitty's lace. Each design, although the same shape, has a different filling stitch, joined at the base with scrolls.

AN OLD BURANO GROUND

Work the foundation row.

1st row *Make two stitches into each of the next two loops, miss two loops and repeat from *.

2nd row Work five stitches into the short loops between the sets of two stitches of row 1.

3rd row Work one stitch into each loop of the five stitches of row 2.

4th row Working over the long loops of the previous three rows, *make two buttonhole stitches, leave a small space and work another two stitches into the same loop. Take the thread over to the next set of three long loops and repeat from *.

Rows 2, 3 and 4 make up the pattern.

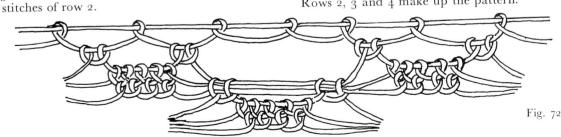

Fig. 72

A GROUND FROM PARAGUAY

Work a foundation row of buttonhole stitches across the space.

1st row   Miss seven loops and make a buttonhole stitch into the next loop, miss seven loops and make a stitch into the next loop and continue across the row.

2nd row   Into each long loop work seven stitches.

3rd row   Into the short loop between groups of seven stitches, work two buttonhole stitches, work one stitch each side of the centre stitch in the groups of seven and repeat to end of row.

4th row   Make two stitches to the left of the stitches in centre of group, make one in loop between the two stitches, then two more to the right of centre. Miss the next two stitches and repeat.

5th row   Make a long loop under the stitches just formed in row 4, then work two stitches in the loop between the groups directly under the blocks of two formed in row 2.

The pattern starts again with row 2.

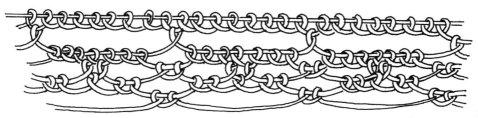

Fig. 73

Samplers of stitches worked from the cuff from Paraguay shown overleaf.

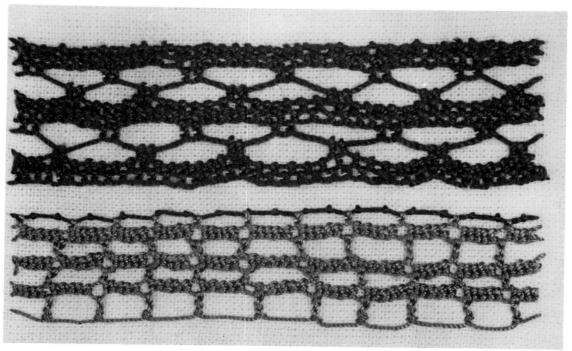

89

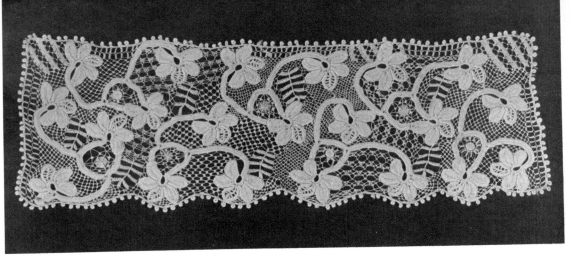

One of a pair of cuffs from Paraguay.

A modern design worked by Pat Gibson from the samplers of stitches worked from the cuff from Paraguay using silk threads ranging in sizes from 80/3 to 130/3.

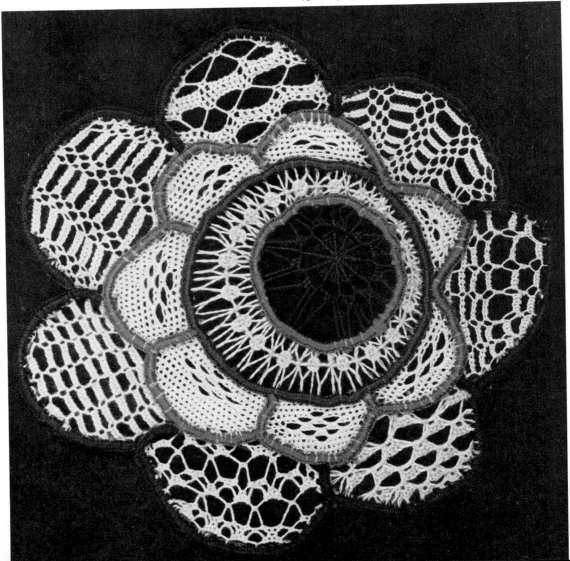

Samples of stitches worked from the cuff from
Paraguay.

Samplers of stitches worked from the cuff from Paraguay.

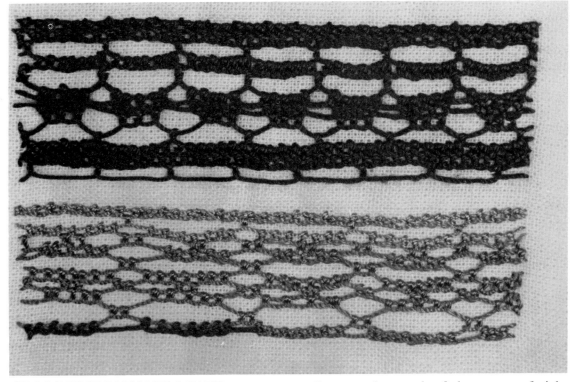

GROS POINT DIAMONDS GAZE QUADRILLÉE

Work a sample piece over thirty-seven stitches, with a cordonnette down each side to anchor the ends of each row. When working a piece of lace, arrange the first diamond in a central position, stitches will be added or omitted from the design as necessary. Work the foundation row from right to left, then continue as follows:

1st row Miss the first two loops, make a stitch into each of the next three loops, *miss two loops, work one stitch into each of the eight loops, miss two loops and work one stitch into each of the next three loops, repeat from * to end of row.

2nd row Work one stitch into the first loop, miss two loops, work one stitch into the next three loops. Miss the next two, *work three stitches into the first long loop, two stitches into the groups of three, then three stitches into the next long loop. Miss two loops, work one stitch into the next three loops, which should be the centre stitches of the group of eight, miss two loops and repeat from *.

3rd row This row is made up of groups of thirteen stitches, divided by two loops. Make three stitches into the loops each side of the groups of eight, as

well as one into each of the groups of eight, making thirteen stitches.

Miss two loops, make three stitches into the next long loop to start the group of thirteen stitches again.

4th row Make three stitches into the first long loop. Miss two loops to bring the next eight stitches directly below the group of eight in row 2. *Miss the next two loops, make three stitches into the long loop, miss two loops, work one stitch into the next eight loops and repeat from *.

5th row Make one stitch at the beginning of the row. Miss two loops which should bring the next stitches into the centre of the eight on the previous row. *Work one stitch into the centre three stitches of the group of eight. Miss two loops, work three stitches into the long loop, make one stitch into each of the next two loops and three stitches into the next long loop. Miss two loops and repeat from *.

6th row Work as for row 3, making the thirteen stitches by working three stitches into the loop each side of the group of eight stitches, leave two loops and make the next group of thirteen.

A diamond of holes can be worked within each

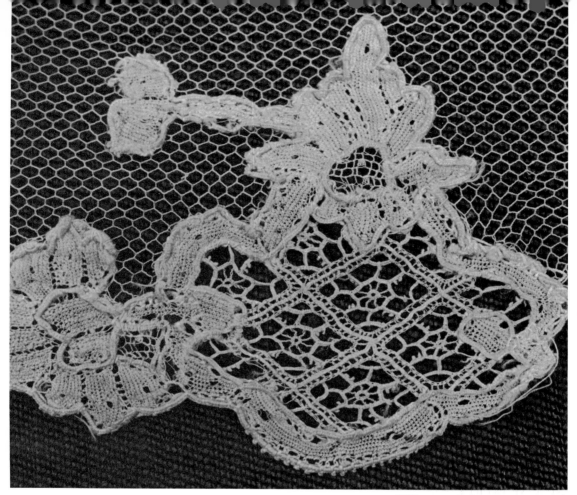

Fillings worked on a square mesh.

of the solid diamond shapes in the following manner:

In the group of eight stitches, work three, miss two and work three.

In the group of thirteen, work four, miss two, work one, miss two, work four.

GENOA LACE STITCH

1st row   Work four buttonhole stitches, *miss the space of three stitches then work three, miss the space of three and work four. Continue across the space from *.

2nd row   Make nine stitches, three into the loops each side of the cluster of four of the previous row and three into the loops of the four. Miss three stitches and work another nine as before.

3rd row   Make nine stitches, three into the last three loops of the nine stitches on the previous row, three into the long loop and three into the first three loops of the next block of nine. Miss three and repeat.

4th row   This is worked as the first row, making the three stitches into the long loop and the four stitches are made into the centre loop of the blocks of nine.

SPANISH GROUND

Those new to Point de Sorrento stitch should work a sample first as follows:

Lay a foundation row.

Into the first loop work a buttonhole stitch, then take the needle back over the loop and bring the needle through the loop of the stitch just made. This stitch must not be pulled tight when being worked.

1st row Work three Sorrento stitches, leave the space of three stitches, work another group of three, the thread between the groups is kept straight. Twist down the side of the space to the depth of one stitch.

2nd row Work two stitches into the loops of the groups of three stitches on the previous row, leaving a loop between each pair of threads. Twist down the side of the space to the depth of two stitches.

These two rows form the ground, the first of the rows being worked into the loops between the pairs on row 2.

Fig. 74

BRUGGE FILLING

This filling is a square mesh, but instead of the threads being laid first and having the fillings worked into them, the mesh is made as the lace progresses.

1st row Lay the thread from one side of the space being filled to the other and make a knot stitch to avoid the thread from becoming slack. Then make a stitch into the cordonnette directly below the knot.

2nd row Calculate where the intersections will be made and make a buttonhole stitch between the intersections. Having made the first buttonhole stitch on the laid thread make two Point de Venise at the point of crossing. Make a buttonhole stitch on the laid thread before making the next two Point de Venise. Continue across the space and make a knot stitch into the cordonnet before whipping down to the start of the next laid thread, which should be the distance between that of the two pairs of Point de Venise.

Lay the pairs of thread in one direction to cover the space, following the instructions for rows 1 and 2.

Now cross these threads as follows:

Take the thread through the centre of the pairs of Point de Venise stitches and on reaching the opposite side make a knot stitch, then make the stitch into the cordonnet directly below the knot as in row 1.

On the return row make the buttonhole stitch between the crossings. At the intersections weave around the threads to form a wheel.

94

Antique piece shows the use of rings and needlepoint
lace inserted into fine muslin.

FILLINGS USING A SQUARE MESH

It is best to work all these fillings on a large scale with a fairly coarse thread, ideally using a $\frac{1}{4}$ inch (6 mm) mesh and 100 crochet cotton. Once mastered it is easy to work down in scale with fine thread to get the effect found in old lace.

There are a number of fillings worked on a square mesh, so save time by laying a fairly large area and work a little of each filling on the same practice piece. Mount in the usual way onto backing material and lay a cordonnet all around. Then lay and couch a cordonnet to form blocks. Each block will then hold a different filling.

To lay the mesh, lay the first set of threads across the area $\frac{1}{4}$ inch (6 mm) apart, then lay the second set of threads at right angles, knotting at each crossing.

Sampler showing stitches given in the book, particularly chequered spiders.

CHEQUERED SPIDERS

Lay the square foundation, allowing enough space for ten buttonhole stitches to each side of the squares. Anchor to the base material at each intersection. This may seem time-consuming, but it saves counting the stitches and makes for ease in working them on the short sides of the squares.

1st row   Work ten buttonhole stitches into the top of the first square, pass the needle behind the vertical thread, and work ten stitches into the next square. Continue to work ten stitches into each square across the space.

2nd row   Turn the work around and work back along the same line of mesh by passing the needle behind the cordonnet at the beginning of the row and working ten stitches into the first square, making one stitch between each stitch made in the first row. Take the needle behind the vertical and along to the next square. Make ten stitches into each square as in row 1.

Whip down the cordonnet to the next line of squares of the mesh and repeat rows 1 and 2.

Continue in this way until all the horizontal lines have the two rows of buttonhole stitches worked.

Next turn the mesh to work the vertical lines of the squares in the same way, working ten stitches into each square as given for the first and second rows.

Each square is now to be filled with a woven ring as follows:

Starting at the top right-hand corner of the first square, take the thread across to the bottom left-hand corner.

Whip along five loops to the bottom centre stitch and take the thread up to the top centre loop.

Whip along five stitches to the left-hand top corner and take the thread down to the bottom corner.

Whip up the right-hand side of the square to centre loop, then take the thread across to the left-hand side.

Twist along the thread just laid to the centre of the square and make a knot stitch over all laid threads to make a central point.

Now work the ring by going over one thread, under the next two threads and back over one until half the square is filled.

Stop working the ring at the right-hand top of the square, then take the thread behind the ring just made and out at the bottom left-hand leg of

96

the ring. Twist down to the join of the second square.

Start the ring of the second square by working from the bottom right-hand corner to the top left-hand corner and reverse the instructions given for the first square.

Continue to work in this way along the line of the square, then whip down the cordonnet to the second row of squares.

CHEQUERED RINGS

Lay the square foundation, allowing enough space for ten buttonhole stitches to each side of the squares. Anchor to the base material at each intersection, then work the two rows of buttonhole stitches as given for the foundation of chequered spiders.

To work the rings, make a buttonhole stitch into the top right-hand corner of the first square, then continue around as follows. One stitch into the centre loop of the right, down to the bottom right-hand corner, to the centre loop on the bottom, then to the left-hand bottom corner. Now come up the left side, make a stitch into the centre

Antique piece showing use of square mesh filling using chequered rings.

left loop, then into the top left corner, to the centre top loop and over to the first stitch.

Whip around the loops of the stitches just made, and pull up to form a ring. Continue to whip around the ring and give a base for the working of the stitches; three or four times should be enough.

Over the ring work buttonhole stitches. The number of stitches will depend on the size of the thread being used and the size of the ring.

Continue to work the rings in the same order as the directions given for the chequered spiders.

CHEQUERED RINGS WITH PICOTS

Lay the square foundation and work the two rows of buttonhole stitches over the mesh as given for chequered spiders.

Into each square, make a buttonhole stitch from the top right corner to bottom right corner. Then from bottom left corner to top left corner and over to the first stitch.

97

Antique filling showing another version of chequered rings.

Whip over the four loops three or four times to make the base for the rings, as given for the chequered rings.

Buttonhole over the ring to the centre of the right side, then form a picot. Continue around the ring to the centre of the bottom quarter and make another picot. Work around the ring making the next two picots in the same way.

Continue to work the rings in the same order as given for the chequered rings.

ELECIA FILLING

The foundation for this filling is laid in groups of three with $\frac{1}{4}$ inch (6 mm) space between groups.

1st row   Lay three threads, leaving a space of one thread between each. Leave a $\frac{1}{4}$ inch (6 mm) space then lay the next three threads. Continue in this way across space.

2nd row   Cross with a second set of threads, laid in the same order and spacing. Knot the threads of alternate groups at each crossing, i.e. knot three, miss three, knot three.

3rd row   Cross diagonally, making sure the thread is lying across the exact middle of the untied threads of the previous row.

4th row   This is another set of diagonal threads laid over the last set but knotting together at the centre all the threads of the three previous rows. See the diagram. These are the alternate crossings that so far have been left loose.

This forms the foundation.

To work the flower motifs whip down one of the diagonal threads to a group of sixteen threads. Weave on two of these threads until almost reaching the little square of knotted threads. Take the needle through the weaving, back down to the centre and weave another two strands. Continue in this way until eight petals have been formed.

Whip diagonally down to the next group of sixteen threads and work the next flower as shown in the diagram.

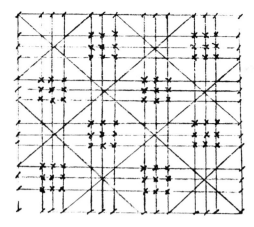

Fig. 75

A sampler worked by Pat Gibson showing Elecia filling and wheel insertion.

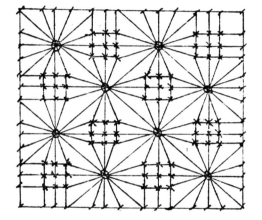

Fig. 76

Elecia filling.

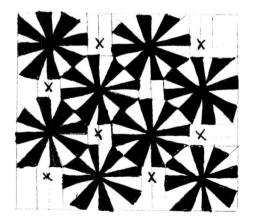

Fig. 77

Fig. 78

Katie's kisses.

KATIE'S KISSES

Lay a foundation as given for the Elecia filling, rows 1, 2, 3 and 4.

Starting at the centre of the tied groups of sixteen threads weave on three of these threads until reaching the knotted threads. Slip the needle down through the weaving back to the centre.

Weave the next three threads until reaching another set of knotted threads, take the needle back through the weaving to the centre. Repeat until all four sections have been woven.

Whip down to the diagonal thread to the centre of the next group of sixteen knotted threads and repeat.

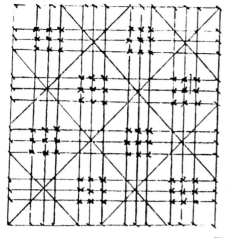

Fig. 79

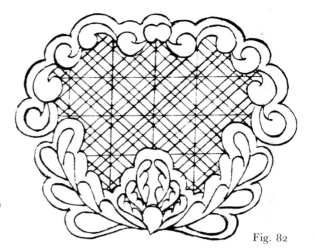

Fig. 82

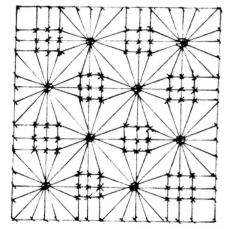

Fig. 80

Fig. 81

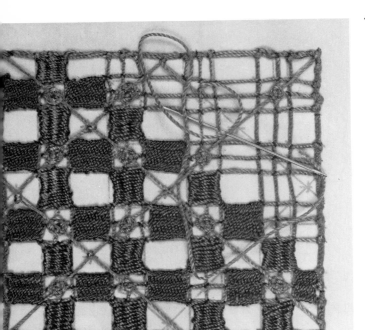

Trellis filling.

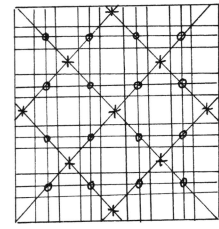

Fig. 83

TRELLIS FILLING

Lay the foundation as given for Elecia filling rows
1 and 2, knotting the threads at each crossing.

To work the filling, start at the bottom left-
hand corner and weave over the first three
upright threads, until reaching the knots.

Then weave the three horizontal threads on the
row above and to the right. Work as far as the next
set of knots.

Work in this order across the diagonal, then
turn the work around and work along the next set
of three upright threads and across the work to the
next corner.

The diagonal threads are worked after the
woven bars are complete.

Knot the thread to the cordonnet, take it
across to the first crossed threads in the centre of
four woven bars and knot at the cross. Counting
the thread just laid and the cross, there are five
threads on which to work a woven ring.

Continue across the diagonal and work a
woven ring in the centre of each block of four
woven bars.

On the second diagonal, the thread is knotted
on passing the first diagonal and the intermediate
woven rings are worked.

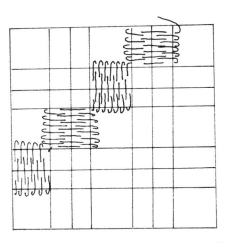

Fig. 84

TUDOR ROSE

Lay a foundation of squares $\frac{1}{4}$ inch (6 mm) apart with single thread.

Then cross diagonally with double threads laid side by side.

Cross diagonally in the opposite direction first with a single thread, then lay another thread in the same way, but knot the twelve threads together where they cross.

Weave a petal over three threads, taking one of the double threads, the single thread and one from the next pair of diagonals.

Take the needle through the centre of the weaving to the middle and make another petal on the next three threads, one from the pair of diagonal threads, a single and one from the next pair.

Make four petals to each rose.

Twist along to the next twelve threads, knotting the set of four as you pass.

Tudor rose.

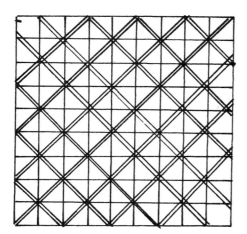

Fig. 85

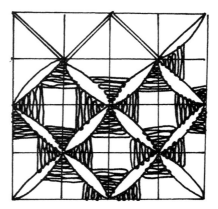

WHEELS

There are many ways in which wheels can be worked and just as many ways in which these fillings can be used. They can be used, with advantage, to fill an asymmetric space or can become an integral part of the design. In Point de Gaze, they are used in sequence in the form of arcs, making a very effective edging.

A number of differently worked wheels in sequence can be used for a dress trim if worked on a large scale. By working a series of wheels, joining up first into lengths then into blocks, a large area can be built up.

The first thing is to decide on the size of wheel to be worked and draw this on paper. Cover with a piece of acetate film and tack to the foundation material. This is all explained in detail in the chapter on working methods in the book *The Technique of Needlepoint Lace*. The threads used will depend on the size of the wheel to be worked, the smaller the diameter of the wheel, the finer the threads.

To work an individual wheel, it is necessary to lay a foundation thread, which is couched around the circle. Most centres are woven, over and under each thread if there is an uneven number of rays, or under two back over one, then under the next two if the rays are of an even number. The latter forms spines radiating out from the centre and if this effect is preferred it can be worked on an uneven number of threads also.

If the thread is taken across the centre of the circle from one side to the other, then the wheel will finish with an even number of rays radiating out from the centre. To get an uneven number of rays, take the thread across just off centre to start, then the last ray to be laid will bring back a centre point. It is always advisable to mark in the position of the points of the rays on the design. Having taken the thread from one side to the other whip along the couched ring to the position

of the next ray. Now cross the already laid thread and anchor the working thread to the opposite edge with a knot stitch. Whip along the circle to the position of the next rays and repeat. Continue in this way until the circle is complete. If working the uneven number of threads, the last ray will go from the outside edge down to the centre point. Here all threads can be pulled together with a buttonhole stitch worked across the centre, the needle is then brought up through the centre and the weaving is started from that point. When working an even number of threads, it is best to finish off the rays at the outside edge and start with a new thread at the centre. Again, as for the first method, make a buttonhole stitch over the centre threads, bring the needle up through the centre and start by taking the needle under two threads, back over one thread, then forward under the next two threads. Work at least three rows before cutting off the tail at the start of the new thread in the centre.

To fill an asymmetric space, lay in the rays as before, regardless of the shape. Work the wheel at the point where the rays cross. The remaining area can be filled with either Brussells, Point de Venise or whichever stitch is in keeping with the lace being worked, incorporating the odd ray or two into the filling.

A long narrow space can be filled with a wheel insertion. This works on the straight or will happily follow curves. The same foundation is used for the wheel and the star motif.

A sampler worked by Pat Gibson showing all the wheels in this book.

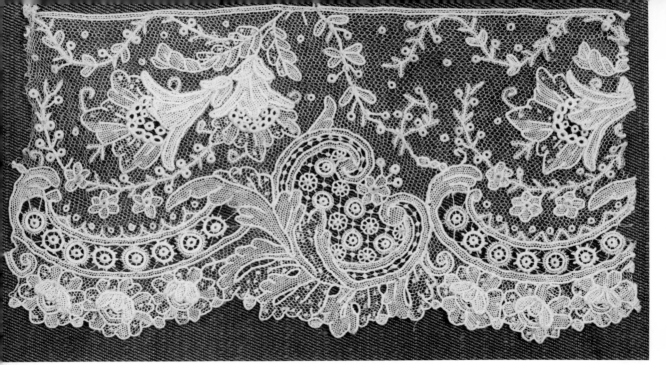

Piece of Point de Gaze showing the use of wheels in
sequence in the form of arcs forming the integral
part of the design.

WHEEL INSERTION

Couch two parallel lines the length needed for the
space being filled.

Work a series of 'herringbone' stitches, widely
spaced, along the couched threads. Turn the work
around and return, making the next row of
stitches between those of the previous row.

To work the third row, whip along the top
couched thread until reaching the spot where two
threads form a cross. Make a straight stitch down
to the bottom line. Make a knot stitch, then whip
along the bottom couched thread to the next set of
crossed threads. Here the working thread is taken
back up to the top couched thread and knotted.
Repeat along the row of 'herringbone' stitches.

The last row of foundation threads is laid right
through the centre of the previous rows making a
knot at the centre of each cross.

To work the wheels, whip along the last laid
thread to the centre of the first group of threads.
Take the needle under two threads and back over
one, then under the next two threads, keeping the
working thread down firmly toward the centre of
the wheel.

Repeat until half of the thread between this
wheel and the next has been covered.

Next whip along the centre thread to the next
set of crossed threads and make the next wheel.

WHEEL NO. 2

Lay eight rays and work a woven wheel. When
weaving on an even number of rays work over two
rays at the start of each round. This particular
wheel needs about ten rounds.

Twist up one of the rays a short distance and
knot firmly for the start of the next ring. Pass to
each ray in turn making sure the knot is tight on
each ray till arriving back at the first knot. Work
around this ring, whipping twice into every space.

Into each space work four buttonhole stitches,
take the thread back and work a buttonhole stitch
between the first and second of these stitches. On
the loop just made work six buttonhole stitches to
form a picot. Work the following seven spaces in
the same way.

Twist up the next ray to the outside of the circle
then along the couched thread to the centre
between two rays.

Take the working thread down to between two
picots, anchor to the ring, then back to the outside
edge between the next two rays. Continue around
the wheel.

Now work an equal number of buttonhole
stitches on each thread just laid to form eight
points.

Elongated wheels used round the neckline of
Plastron for a dress. Brussels, late nineteenth century.

106

WHEEL NO. 3

Lay in sixteen rays, twist down one of the rays to the centre and knot firmly. Weave under two, back over one, and under two for several rounds.

Whip two or three times up one of the rays and form a ring as in wheel no. 2.

Weave over and under between two rays ten times. Take the needle down through the woven threads back to the ring and do the same on the next two rays. Repeat until there are eight blocks of weaving.

Knot each ray to form another ring, making sure the knots are close to the woven blocks.

Whip up the nearest ray four times and form another ring, knotting firmly all around.

Starting at the angle between the ring just formed and an upright ray, weave to form a triangle. Continue until the weaving has reached the top outside edge of the circle and along the ring to the next ray.

Start another triangle between the next ray and ring.

WHEEL NO. 4

Lay twelve rays, knot firmly in the centre and weave a small wheel, under two, back over one and under two.

Knot each ray to form a ring as in wheel no. 2. Whip up the next ray so forming a small space, and repeat to form another ring.

Continue weaving to fill half the wheel, then whip up the next ray half-way between the wheel and the outside edge of the circle.

Now knot each ray to form another ring. At each intersection, where the ring crosses a ray, weave a separate little wheel, whipping along the ring to the next intersection.

WHEEL NO. 5

Lay in twelve rays and work a wheel, under two back over one, then under two. Work one third of the space; if a new thread is needed this is the best place to lay it in.

Weave at least three times, over and under, around the outside of this line. To weave on an even number of rays it is necessary to go under two threads at the beginning of each round.

On these last woven threads work close buttonhole stitches to form a raised ring, keeping the same number of buttonhole stitches between each ray.

The next round is one buttonhole stitch be-tween each ray. To do this take the needle behind the ray and through the nearest buttonhole stitch, continue around all twelve spaces. Now work a series of buttonhole stitches over these long loops just made, which will form a row of little scallops between the rays.

Whip the working thread up the nearest ray for about a quarter of its length and make a knot stitch. Continue to make a knot stitch over each ray, then weave once around this new circle. The two threads just woven as a ring are now but-tonholed over. Keeping the same number of stitches between each ray, continue around the twelve spaces.

The next row is formed by taking the thread through the top of the buttonhole stitch of the last row, nearest the ray that has just been reached, then back to the previous ray; take the needle through the buttonhole stitch of the last round. Make three loops between these stitches; over these three loops work an uneven number of buttonhole stitches. Pass to the next ray and repeat until all rays have a worked scallop between them. Neatly fasten off through the back of the stitches.

Join a new thread to the outside circle, whip along until reaching the first scallop, and knot the thread to the outside circle directly above the middle stitch on the scallop. Take the thread down, then through the loop of this centre stitch and whip back to the outside circle. Pull to lift the scallop into an arc.

Whip along the outside of the circle until reaching the point above the centre stitch of the next scallop and repeat. Buttonhole around the outside circle if the wheel is being used as a separate motif. If being incorporated into a piece of lace, the final cordonnette will cover.

WHEEL NO. 6

This wheel is started in a different manner to the previous ones. First draw the outside circle, around which a series of two holes must be marked, one on the outside of the circle, the other directly in line on the inside. Take the couching thread and make short tacking stitches from an inside hole to its corresponding outer one, see the diagram. This was called la Trace, and was worked by the Traceuse before being given over to the Reseleuse or Fondeuse who worked the mesh or grounds.

Now take the working thread and with a ball

An antique tie-end showing various wheels.

point needle proceed to run the thread between the tacking stitches for three or four rounds. Over these laid threads work a round of spaced buttonhole stitches to the inside of the ring, instead of the knots forming on the outside of the ring. Fasten off.

Make a small ring by twisting the working thread either around a knitting needle or a ring stick, five or six times. Loosely whip them all together into a circle and place central to the wheel to form a hub, and tack to the backing material. Divide the wheel and the circle into four equal sections.

Make four rings of five or six turns, nearly large enough to reach from one of the dividing points on the wheel to its opposite number on the hub, and tack into place on the backing material. Make sure they are well secured to the hub and tacked to within a picot of the outside of the wheel.

Starting at the base of the first of these four wheels make five buttonhole stitches, then a loop picot (see Fig. 86) instructions for which are given below.

Loop picot

This is worked from right to left. Work along to the position of the first picot and place a pin either under the foundation threads of the bar and into the base material, or if working on a pillow, stick the pin straight through into the pillow itself. Pass the working thread from right to left under the pin, then still working to the left, over the top of and down behind the bar or foundation threads.

Throw the working thread over the point of the pin to the right.

Make a buttonhole stitch around the picot by taking the working thread under both sides of the loop but over the pin, under the working thread where it emerges from behind the bar, then over the working thread where it is forming the large loop.

Pull tight to form the picot. The spacing of these picots will depend entirely on how and where the picots are being used (even the length of the picots can be varied) to form scallops.

Continue to work five stitches and a picot until reaching the buttonhole stitch that is one of the dividing points. Then work down the other side of the ring, placing picots to correspond with those made on the first side. Work the other three rings in the same way.

Starting at the centre hub, between two worked rings, take the working thread up to the buttonhole stitches on the wheel, within a space of four or five buttonhole loops from the picot holding the ring. Take the needle up and through the next loop and whip over the next loops to within four or five stitches of the picot holding the next ring. Take the working thread down to the

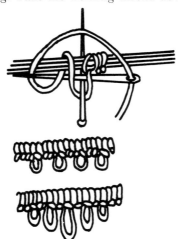

Fig. 86

hub, so forming a triangle. Weaving over and under these threads proceed back up to the wheel. The needle passes through the buttonhole stitch holding the thread and is then taken through the weaving down one side, back to the hub.

Whip around the hub to the point between the next two rings and repeat. Make the next two triangles in the same way.

A couronne is attached to the hub and the cordonnette finishes off the outside of the wheel.

WHEEL NO. 7

Start in the same way as wheel no. 6 as far as dividing the wheel and the hub into four equal sections.

Join the working thread to the hub at a dividing line and take up to the point on the wheel. Take the needle through one buttonhole stitch and back out through its neighbour, then back down to the hub. Do this four times and over these laid threads work an Ardenza Point bar, up to the wheel, through the buttonhole stitches holding the threads, then back to finish the other half of the Ardenza Point bar at the hub. Work three more Ardenza Point bars on the dividing points.

Starting at the centre hub, between two Ardenza Point bars follow the instructions for making the woven triangles given for wheel no. 6. Make one triangle between each bar.

WHEEL NO. 8

Make a small couronne and place as a central hub. Lay a cordonnet of four threads around the outside of the ring. Over the cordonnet work a ring of buttonhole stitches with the loops facing to the centre of the wheel.

Divide the hub into six equal spaces and mark the outside ring off into six equal spaces, placing each mark central to the space on the hub.

Work a loop between each marked space by taking the working thread from the hub to the outside ring, through the loop of the buttonhole stitch at one of the places marked, back to the next marked space on the hub. Take the needle under and over this thread twice before returning back to the next marked space on the outside ring. Continue to make a loop into the next five spaces, making the two twists at the hub each time.

On arriving back at the first loop take the needle under and over the thread twice to put the twist to match the other loops.

Put the point of the needle above the twist and

pull down to tighten the twist, then buttonhole up the outside of the loop. Half-way up the thread work a picot, then continue to the outside of the ring. Make a buttonhole stitch into the same loop as the foundation thread, then work back along the other half of the loop making a picot, to match the one opposite. Place the needle in the twist and make a buttonhole stitch, pulling down toward the hub, to keep the twists equal in length to the first. Repeat around the next five loops in the same way.

An elaborate wheel forming the centre of a flower.

WHEEL NO. 9

Use the trace as given for wheel no. 6, firstly around the outside edge, then two more rings at one-third intervals inside the wheel.

Lay ten rays and knot stitch around the rays to form a ring in the centre. Weave around this ring three times, then buttonhole over the threads to form the hub.

Whip up the nearest ray to the first ring of

'trace' and take the thread around through the trace three times. Work Ardenza stitch over the laid threads, keeping the same number of stitches between each pair of rays and forming the loops of the stitches to the outside of the ring.

Whip up the nearest ray to the second ring of trace and make another ring in the same way, forming the Ardenza stitch directly above the previous row, with the loops forming toward the centre of the rings.

Alençon beads are worked between these two rings.

Whip to the outside edge of the ring and take the thread through the trace four times to form a thick foundation. Over this foundation work a ring of Ardenza Point bar.

Working on the outside loops of the Ardenza stitches make seven buttonhole stitches into each loop to form small scallops. Then work five buttonhole stitches into the inside loops of the stitches to form smaller scallops on the inside of the ring. Finish off by running the working thread through three or four stitches of the trace.

With the new thread run through the second trace to a central point between two rays, take the thread up to an inside scallop of the outside ring and form an Alençon bar back to the second trace. Run the thread through the trace and form an Alençon bar between every other ray, making six bars in all.

CARE OF LACE

Never fold lace as this is the easiest way of ruining net or background material. The best way to store lace is to make a roll of acid-free tissue paper and keep the lace rolled around the tissue. If storing long lengths such as a flounce or wedding veil, find a cardboard box wide enough to take the lace, then line the box with newspaper. This helps to keep moths at bay as they dislike printer's ink. Cover the newspaper with tissue paper and lay the first layer of the flounce on the bottom of the box. Make parcels of newspaper covered with tissue paper the length and width of the box and lay a parcel of paper between each layer of lace, laying the lace back and forth on itself, concertina fashion.

Heirlooms or precious pieces such as christening gowns or baby bonnets should have the tissue crumpled up and placed inside the sleeves or wherever the material is gathered, such as shoulders, cuffs or bodices. Layers of tissue should be placed inside the skirt, then the whole gown rolled up. Bonnets need a ball of tissue inside the crown and laid in boxes rather than being left flat. Never put lace away dirty, as dirt and perspiration will rot the fine threads quicker than age. Before attempting to clean any lace, decide which category the lace comes under. Linen thread is stronger when wet than when dry and as long as there is no horsehair laid in the cordonnette it will take any amount of washing. Some old lace was chemically cleaned and will have rotted away in places; these parts can be cut out and replaced, but before starting on this kind of venture do make sure you have the equivalent threads to do the repair.

The old way of washing a length of narrow lace was to wrap it around a bottle, tacking it in place with fine thread and fine needles, making large stitches that can be easily seen when it comes to removing the lace. Half fill the bottle and cork it, then immerse in a pan of cold water to which good quality soap flakes have been added, add a pinch of soda and bring to the boil. When the water begins to look dirty, place the pan under hot running water until the water in the pan runs clean, then add fresh soap flakes and repeat until the water runs clean. Rinse under running hot water, to avoid cracking the glass bottle. Squeeze the lace by wrapping in a clean towel while still on the bottle, leave for an hour, remove then press while still damp.

Heavy lace should be put in a muslin bag with plenty of room to lie flat. This is because the weight of the water when removing it from the pan could cause untold damage to the lace. By lifting the muslin bag, supporting from below with a plastic fish slice or spatula, straight from the pan to the draining board the water can drain away without damage to the contents.

Old Maltese silk lace is a risk even when washed in luke warm water, so is best left alone; it is also difficult to find the right silk for repair work. The Maltese silk now used for gold embroidery is the wrong colour and texture.

Black lace can have vinegar added to the washing water to help retain the black dye which often turns dark brown when washed. It is important to watch the tip of the iron when pressing lace, since it is so easily pushed through a space or under a bar and can cause a lot of unnecessary damage. Pin any points to shape and keep the angle of the stitches right when pressing. Raised work should be ironed on the wrong side on the soft cloth while still damp. Then turn the lace over and with the rounded end of a spoon handle gently rub up toward the raised work. This helps to put a shine on the surface of the lace, and lifts the raised work. At one time this was done with an instrument called an Afficot.

Never store lace with starch left in it, because

Baby's bonnet showing crown composed mainly of
rings.

Christening gown designed and worked by Shirley
Warren using 130/3 silk thread.

the lace will crack. If lace is to be worn and needs a little stiffening, Tragacanth is ideal. Leave a little Tragacanth to soak in cold water for three hours to allow it to swell up well, then mix with a wooden spoon. Stir it well to form a fairly thick colourless liquid. Leave the lace pinned out on the ironing board and spread the liquid over the lace. Repeat two or three times then allow to dry away from direct heat.

Ecclesiastical laces are likely to get wine stains, especially around the cuffs. Ideally they should be removed at once as old stains will take longer to remove. Hold the stain over a sink and pour water through the lace or put it on a turkish towel, dab it with water until the stains start to remove. The stain may become larger as it weakens down, so start around the outside edge and work in toward the centre of the stain to try and contain it. Any rust marks should be treated with a little boracic powder having dampened the mark with warm soapy water. Lace enjoys a sunbath and a white sheet spread out on the lawn, with the lace laid out on the sheet to soak up the sun works wonders. If it is valuable lace sit with it, in case of birds – the last thing lace needs are birds straight from the pond preening their feathers all over it.

Antwerp thread of the eighteenth century was the finest thread made at that time and any lace made from it is still easy to clean even to this day. Spanish and Italian linen threads are also very strong, mercerized cotton will take any type of soap powder, just beware of any raised or sculptured lace in case of horsehair, Point de Gaze in particular.

Needlepoint lace that has been applied to a net is only as strong as its background. The motifs will be very strong and will stand up to being transferred from the old net to some new. There is a fine cotton net and a pure silk net on the market, both of which will compliment the old point, but do not be tempted to use nylon net, it looks completely out of place.

Before attempting to remove the lace from its backing, draw a full scale pattern of the piece, marking in the shapes and indicating the direction in which they lie. Then turn the design over and draw it up in reverse by laying the drawing against a window pane and tracing over the original design. Mark this side of the paper, stating that it is to be used this side up.

Make a note of any breaks in the lace itself or any missing bars, especially around the edges.

These can be renewed when the lace is applied to the fresh background.

If it is a large project divide the pattern up into manageable pieces, cover with acetate and mount onto backing material in the same way as if starting a new lace.

As the needlepoint lace is removed from its original net, tack it in place on the new pattern upside down, making sure it lays in the right place and also the right direction.

If the pattern has been cut into a number of separate pieces, number each piece i.e. right top corner, left top corner, right bottom corner, left bottom corner. If there is a centre piece also mark that top, bottom left and right. This is very important if it is an asymmetric design. Be very careful how the lace is removed. Work from the back of the original net and snip just one stitch. Turn the work over and carefully lift the lace at that point. Using a long sewing needle or lace pricker, trace the next stitch along that connects the lace to the net and pull the thread gently, making sure that it is the right thread, then pull through. Each pulled stitch will release a fraction more of the lace. When the unpicked thread gets too long cut it off, or it will knot back on itself and can cause some unnecessary snags. When the complete motif is free of the background, tack it into place on the new pattern upside down. When the entire lace has been removed from its original backing and relayed to the new pattern, the new net is laid completely over the lace motifs and each one is appliqued into its right position working from the back. If the pattern was cut up into smaller pieces for easier handling, some of the pattern backing material might need to overlap to bring the lace into its right position. Alternatively each piece can be applied and removed from the paper pattern before laying the next piece into position.

If it is a collar or cuffs that are being repaired a new engrelure will be needed. This can be made of bobbin lace using the cucumber design or it can be worked in needlepoint. The best way to do this is to lay the cordonnet to the size of the neck band and work four or five rows of corded Brussels stitch, then work one row of holes by working into five loops and missing two loops. On the return row, work into the four loops of the previous row and three stitches into the long loops. Then the next four or five rows work into every loop.

Fashion and Lace

With 5 yards (4.60 m) of pure silk brought back from China, a bag of silk threads in a range of pinks, from apple blossom pink, through cerise to carmen, another bag containing silks with every colour in the spectrum, all waiting to be used, the question was how?

A kimono was the answer; they had been around since the Nara period which was between AD 645–742 and had not changed or gone out of fashion when I started writing this book, so there was every chance they would still be fashionable by the time the book was finished.

A firebird was exotic enough to carry the whole range of colours, so the design was drawn and enlarged to be big enough to spread over a large area to distribute the weight. The silk material was so light that there was a tendency to drag the material if a number of small motifs were used.

The time factor put a stop to the even bigger motif at the back hem line, and the weight would have dragged the kimono off the shoulders, so it was decided that embroidery would be lighter and quicker.

A peacock in needlelace took up residence on the front. The design around the neck is taken from the DMC book of Chinese embroideries but instead of being worked in the traditional way, it was worked as a piece of needlepoint lace, then applied.

Any embroidery design can be adapted to needlepoint lace, but bear in mind that there is no background material to conveniently stitch through at an awkward point. All threads are carried on the surface, started and ended along a cordonnet.

The pomegranate of fertility opens and releases a hundred offspring. In the DMC book, the design is worked as a traditional Chinese embroidery using stem stitch, buttonhole, long and short, French knots and oriental stitch. This last stitch is worked in long vertical satin stitches which cover the whole surface of a certain part of a design. Horizontal threads are then laid across the vertical threads at regular spaces and couched.

To use as needlepoint lace, the design would be mounted on to the backing material and the cordonnet laid, then corded Brussels stitch used for all leaves and stems, ring stitch couronnes for the seeds or work the area in pea stitch variation. Treble corded Brussels stitch instead of oriental stitch. A couronne with scallops for the bract at the top of the pomegranate.

In the late 1860s and early 1870s fashion looked back for inspiration to the eighteenth century. Now in our century, the idea of an overskirt and a jacket of lace is being taken straight out of a fashion plate of the 1860s. The jackets or *jaquettes* were known as Don Carlos, the zouave, bolero or paletot and each was quite different from the other. About the year 1790 separate jackets became very fashionable and were called baracos. At the same time a short overdress known as a fourneau, which was a pinafore or apron, trimmed all around with a broad flounce, also became popular. Throughout the whole of the first part of the nineteenth century a sleeved over-apron or robe en tablier was worn. Then came the spencer, a short jacket with long sleeves, worn over the dress. By the middle of the century lace was again in favour and was lavishly used as trimming. Some flounces were $9\frac{3}{4}$–12 inches (250–305 mm) deep and four or five layers were used to make up the skirt. A flounce of 20–24 inches (500–600 mm) was not unusual. Needless to say the skirt was lined with stiff gauze and numerous starched white petticoats were worn underneath. The dresses of the second half of the nineteenth century were usually double skirted and for evening wear the overskirt would be made entirely of lace.

Fig. 87

Fig. 88

Fig. 89a
The finished design. The Firebird was enlarged to distribute the weight evenly across the shoulders.

Fig. 89b

There was a period when black lace was embellished with jet beads. It was during this period that the vogue for ecru lace led to pieces of lace being steeped in tea to acquire the dark creamy colour. This fashion reappeared at regular intervals right through to the beginning of this present century and old lace turns up today still bearing the signs of having been dipped in tea. Heavier types of lace gained popularity and the Burano and Youghal needlepoint, with the imitations of Venetian designs, were reaching the market. There was the Point de Gaze lace with the lovely shading of the finely drawn leaves and flowers and the scrolls that were filled with very beautiful wheels. These designs, where a long panel was needed down the two edges at the front, which could be carried around the skirt as small sprays, were ideal for overskirts. At this period, the effect of the double and triple relief of the petals contrasted wonderfully with the extremely delicate needle-made mesh used for the ground. This mesh was made of buttonhole stitch worked in very fine thread, having no addition of cording or whipping, and was worked down to meet the pattern, the join being concealed by small sprigs or trailing leaves. The last century produced lace designs made purposely for the bolero or jacket fashionable at that time and these patterns, stamped onto blue linen, can still be found. The bolero shape in the diagram is from a pattern such as this. It looks impossible but when the shoulders are joined and the darts sewn together at the waist it is complete. It is designed in such a way that it can be worn with or without the little cap sleeves, which were tied inside the armhole with very fine tape in five places. The collar was worn in the same way as a necklace would be worn today, quite apart from the blouse or top that went with the underskirt. Up to this point white, black and ecru were the only colours of lace worn. With the overskirt and waistcoat designs given here any colour can be used to contrast with or complement the dress worn underneath. The floral design could be used for a wedding dress in pristine white over white, but it would take on haute couture style if worked in jewel colours and worn over a black evening dress. The second design is being worked in amethyst, purples and violets, ruby reds from deep crimson to pale rose, the centre of each spiral is in metallic blue and seaweed green with mustard yellow, gold and flashes of white, all on a background of crushed strawberry pink. It is to be

Fig. 89

worn over a pearl coloured silk Lalique style dress. The description of the colours sounds ghastly, but when used together they become quite startling and exciting.

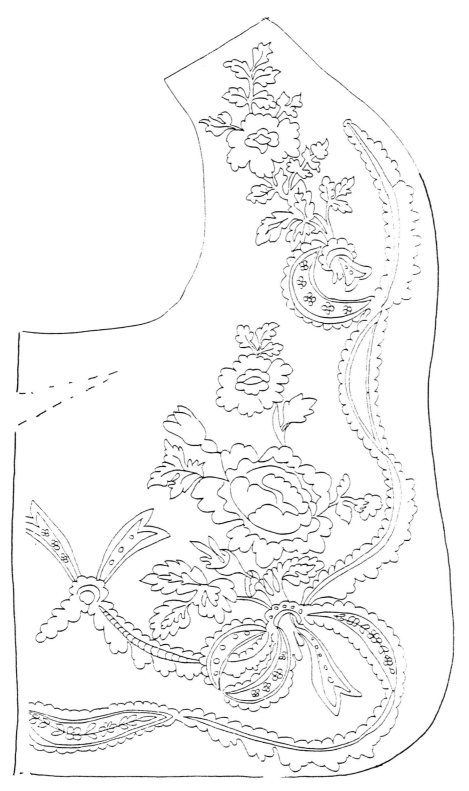

Fig. 90

121

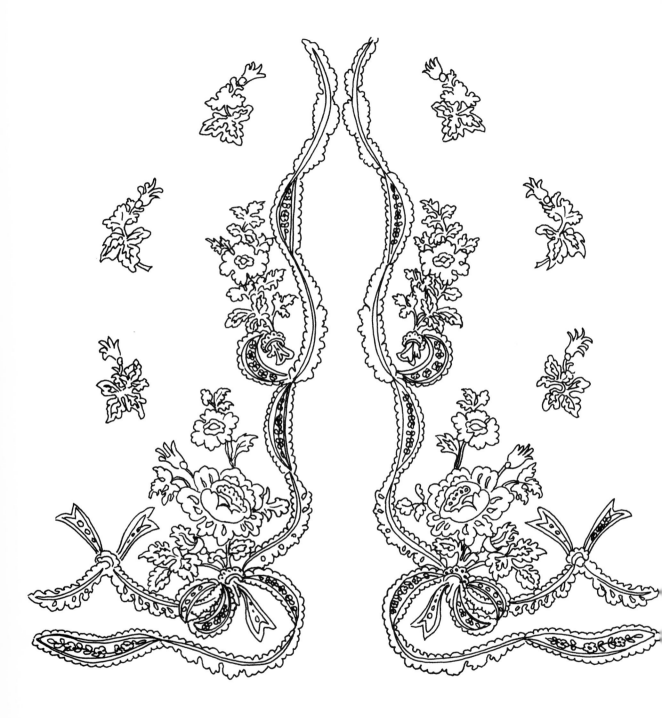

Fig. 91

Pattern for Louave jacket fashionable around the
mid nineteenth century.

Fig. 92

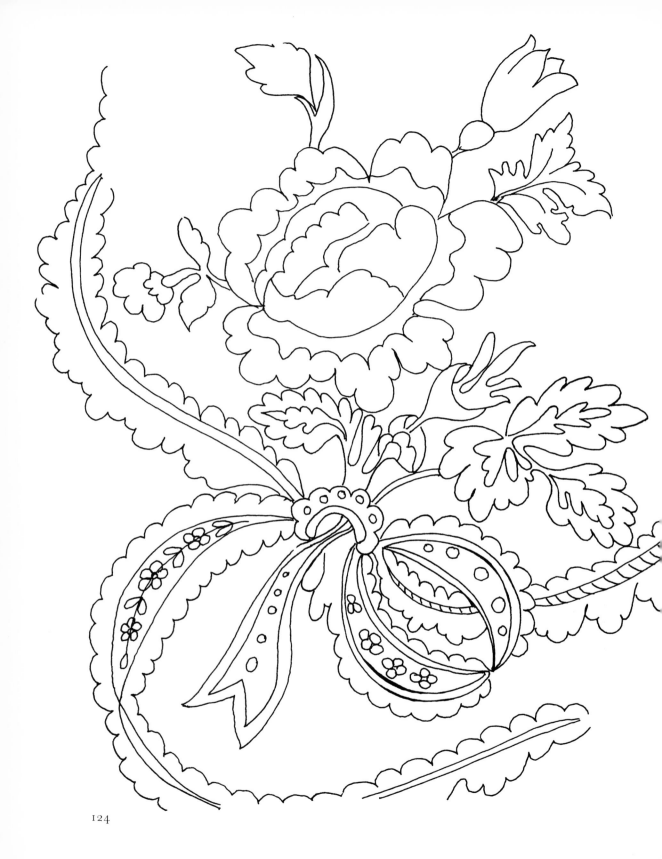

Fig. 93 (left)
Parts of the design for the Floral waistcoat and
overskirt drawn to full size for working. The flower
on the shoulder of the waistcoat is repeated again
above the large spray. The scroll can be mirror-
imaged to join the two sections together.

Fig. 94
The extra motifs used in the design for the overskirt,
drawn to full size. All flower sprays given for the
pattern of the waistcoat are used in conjunction with
this sheet. Extra scrolls are needed to infill, but
tracings can be taken from those already given.

125

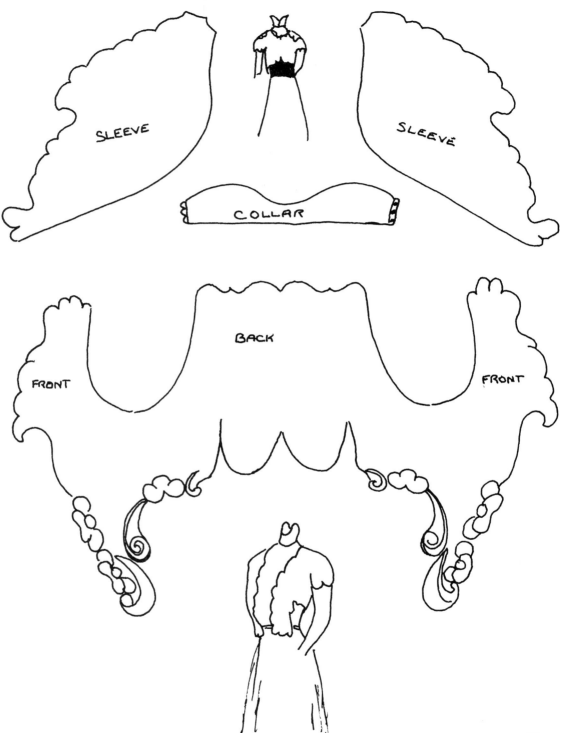

SLEEVE

SLEEVE

COLLAR

BACK

FRONT

FRONT

Fig. 95

Fig. 96

Fig. 97

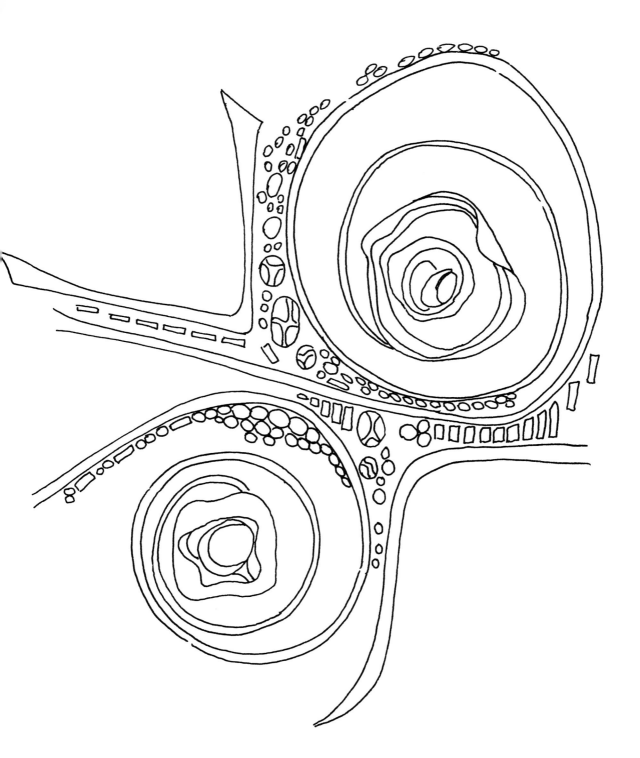

Fig. 98

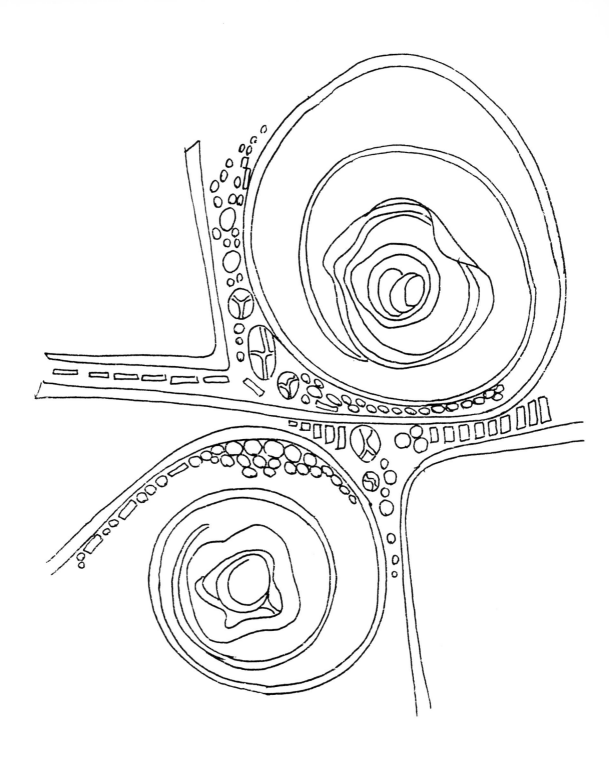

Fig. 99 Motif for centre back of waistcoat and overskirt hemline.

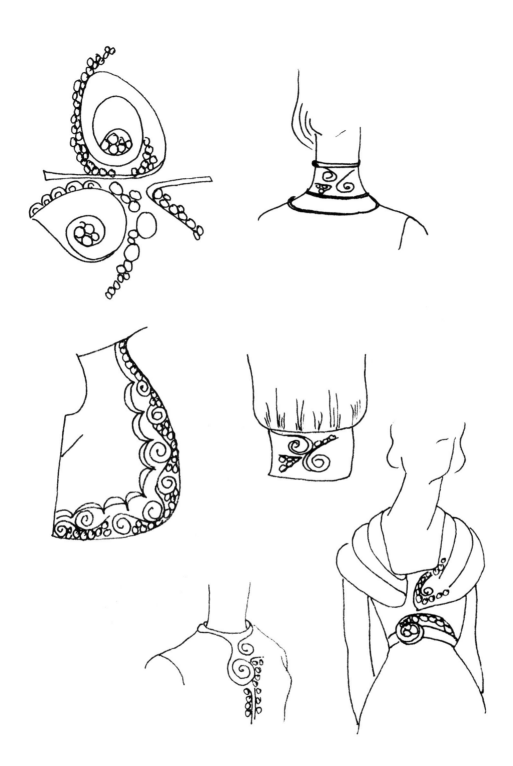

Fig. 100

131

DESIGNING FOR THE CHURCH

Comparatively little needlepoint lace is now made for the Church, more perhaps on the European continent than elsewhere but little in comparison with the amount which was once made both in the convents and by laymen. The Vatican, the Roman Catholic Churches worldwide, the Church of England, the Greek and Russian Orthodox Churches, all have in their possession lace of extraordinary beauty. The very nature of the frequent knotting in needlepoint lace makes it possible for antique specimens to be in a perfect state of preservation.

Before the Reformation in England and to the present day in the Church of Rome, needle-made lace could be found on all the chief vestments. The cassock, amice, alb, girdle, maniple, stole, chasuble, dalmatic, tunic, veil, cape and the surplice all had their share of luxurious lace, sometimes edged with it, and often made entirely from this priceless form of fabric. Some of the original Burano Point lace made from flax threads is almost as stiff as fine card. It has the arabesque design, so much used by the early designers, and has the natural golden shine of pure linen before being treated and bleached white.

Lace, using the term as we now understand it, was first worn in the sixteenth century, rapidly developed in skill and artistic design during the Renaissance period and reached the height of its beauty in the seventeenth century. It is sad that, at the climax of its perfection, it was overtaken by its sister lace, made with the bobbins at a much faster rate, which was therefore so much cheaper to produce. The beautiful specimens that remain in museums and private collections as well as those belonging to the Church must be the inspiration for the future.

Never again will the natural threads, except for silk, be spun as fine as were those early linens, nor be as strong, because of the chemicals used in their production both in growing and manufacture. Man-made threads have yet to prove themselves over a century or two, but the pure silk filament can still be thrown. 'Ultra Fine' thread can be ordered from Leonie Cox in sixty different colours, a natural tussore colour in TW2 and pure white in a 130/3. All of these threads have been tried and proved themselves to be comfortable to work with. If the Ultra Fine is rather difficult the 130/3s will be easier to manage. Needles, too, are the bane of the lives of all needlelace makers. The ball points are too thick for the very fine work, the finest sewing needles split the thread, but enquiries are under way and there is hope of finding special needles better suited to the work.

Not all lace has to be worked in these fine threads; 100 crochet cotton makes a substantial lace that stands up well to modern soap powders and washing machines, but it would be wrong to work in a thick thread a design drawn for minute stitches, without first bringing the design up in comparable size to the proposed thread. Most lace for apparel can be worked in threads equivalent to the 100 or 150 crochet cotton. For things on a smaller scale such as chalice veil, DMC Alsace 60 or 100/3 sewing silk is ideal.

Before embarking on any work for the Church, do make sure that your gift will be accepted. Once that is established, the design can follow through any embroidery or carving already in situ or can take some form of symbolism.

If requested to construct something on a large scale, don't panic; remember that lace designs can be broken down to pieces of manageable size, which are put together when the parts are finished. There can always be schemes for group projects, each lace maker working on an area where her skill is put to the best use. There is nobody to take the place of the 'saint' who offers to do the couching. On a large scale it is tedious to

the extreme, but it has to be done. One way of overcoming this difficulty is to use the sewing machine, see page 76 of *The Technique of Needle-point Lace*, the article contributed by Dorothy McComb of New Zealand. If a co-operative project is undertaken, one person must take overall charge, especially where the workers involved are not together in a group. The overall tensions have to be kept constant, the finished pieces have to be collected together for safe keeping and a word of encouragement or praise given where desirable.

If working with white thread, colours already

A design taken from a stained glass window, worked by Pat Gibson, the thick cordonnette representing the leads, and using the colours from the stained glass.

established in the Church are not going to prove a problem. But by using the gradation of colours, as given in chapter 3 in the section on colour, tints and shades can all be matched to any fabrics that have slightly faded, so that the new does not stand out against the old.

The solid parts of any design are worked in corded stitch and can be taken out of context and worked quite independently. So, bearing this in

Detail of chalice veil made by Lady Town, using a
vine design, which is traditional decoration for altar
linen, featuring the dove and a chalice in the corner.

Chalice veil made by the author in Gütermanns
100/3 silk thread. The silver and gold chalice was
made by Neil Lovesey, member of the Guild of
Master Craftsmen. A diagram of this pattern is
shown on page 35, Fig. 27.

mind, part of the design in a stained glass window, the tiles or carpet on the floor, the ceiling, or, as already mentioned, any carving, can have that design 'lifted' and translated as the basis of the design for the lace.

The focal point in many Churches is the pulpit fall. With a modern design worked boldly in the Venetian style of raised work, it could look impressive and would be totally different from the usual fall, while certainly within the scope of any lacemaker who has worked her way through this book.

The stonework or woodcarving on some pulpits is a work of art in itself and the needlelace maker is in the position of being able to copy the design in miniature so that it will resemble ivory. When the flat areas are worked in off-white and the raised parts in cream, it gives a fair imitation of ivory. This would complement the carving on the pulpit without overpowering it and any congregation that had sat through the years looking at the average drab Victorian pulpit fall would sit up

An altar cloth in needlepoint lace for Wells Cathedral worked by Lady Town, in memory of her daughter who died on active service in India in 1944 at the age of 21 years. The work was begun in 1958 and completed in 1966, taking between 7000 and 8000 hours. For most of the work linen thread of 150 counts was used; 200 thread was used for the net work and the Saints' robes; 250 thread for the Saints' faces, and 300 for the cherubs. At one end of the design stand St John and St Paul, and at the other end St Peter and St Clement.

and take notice. An extra bonus is that it can be kept clean.

Needlelace can be as exciting as any embroidery. If the cross design shown in Fig. 101 is worked in corded stitch, then the shaped couronne in the centre will need to be raised to three or four levels. An open stitch needs to be used for the circle behind the cross, then a gold cord lightly couched around the perimeter to give a distinct outline. Alternatively the cross could be

135

Fig. 101

Fig. 102

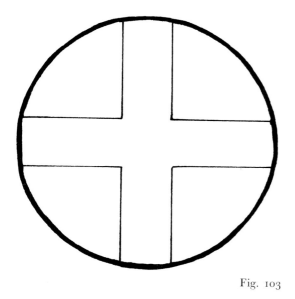

Fig. 103

suspended by fine wire to an outside ring or have a very open work ground as a backing. If this design was to be used on a large scale, it would be easier to work broken down into small sections then built up as each part was completed.

There are numbers of different crosses that have been used through the centuries and the following are easily incorporated into designs for needlelace. The Calvary or Passion Cross could be sculptured and couronnes added to lift it away from the background which again would be worked in any of the more openwork fillings or grounds. This cross falls below the circle while the Greek Cross is contained within it. Any cross can be worked in nature's colours to represent wood or bark, the knots in the wood being formed by either raised work or wheels, which if enclosed within couronnes are given more depth. A mitred joint in the wood can be imitated by working each of the sections of the cross separately, working one end of each section to a 45° point and joining them together, see diagram.

Flowers, birds, fish all form part of the symbolism of the Church. The three fishes, which symbolize baptism, can be worked into many different designs, the fishes having different stitches to give different textures. If applied or inlaid into an embroidery a different dimension is given to the work. This could be useful to start a small project, as three people working with varying tensions could use their favourite stitches to complete one fish each; these would then be brought together without the trouble of trying to keep tensions the same.

Amongst the birds used in the Church, there is the peacock, the emblem of the mortal exchanged for the immortal, the dove which symbolizes the Holy Spirit and Peace, the cock the symbol of St Peter and of repentance, the eagle for the resurrection, it represents triumph over death and is the symbol of St John.

Of the plants and flowers, the best known is the vine, the symbol of the Redeemer. A design using grapes and vine leaves can be built up in the same way as the instructions given for the wedding veil, each complete design section drawn to an exact measurement such as would fit the size of a Laudian or throw-over cloth. Often the wheat is incorporated into a design using the vine. Wheat or corn have the same meaning, the source of life, and is the symbol of the Eucharist. Passion flowers can be found in a great deal of old lace; legend

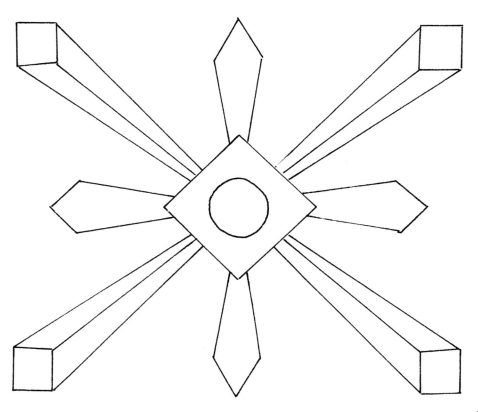

Fig. 104

The Crosses of St George and St Andrew superimposed to give a design suitable for a burse and veil or the ends of a stole. If being worked in conjunction with embroidery on material the squares could be of kid. Alternatively, couronnes could be built up and used to lift the design if it was being used for application.

maintained that the ten petals represent the Apostles, minus two, the one who betrayed and the one who denied; the petals also stand for the Ten Commandments. The centres represent the crown of thorns, and the three pistils and stamens stand for the three wise virgins with their lamps. The pomegranate represents the Tree of Life and the Church, while the snowdrop and the lily both symbolize purity and innocence. The snowdrop is dedicated to the Virgin Mary in the Catholic Church. Another lily, the Crown Imperial, stands for sovereignty. The columbine represents the Holy Spirit and the tulip is the emblem of the chalice and the Holy Grail. Thorns are for tribulation, the bay or laurel and the ivy were

omens of destruction and death. Last but not least on this list of flowers is the olive, standing for peace and goodwill.

All these were used by the early designers of lace, even when the work was not meant to be used especially for the Church. When designing anything connected with the Church do check that the symbolism is right for the particular purpose. Ivy leaves would not be the right choice for a wedding veil for instance.

Colours have to be chosen with care. Lace is white, or has been until now, but colour is creeping in and there is no reason why it should not be used in the Church. So it is as well to be sure where and what colour can be used. White symbolizes God, innocence, purity of thought and the holiness of life. Cream, unbleached linen or natural wild silk was used for Lent and still is in some cases. Gold or yellow symbolizes sovereignty, love, constancy, dignity, wisdom and is used for the Feast of Confessors. Be very careful in the choice of red. Blood red is used for the Feast of

A pall for St Clement Danes made by Lady Town in 1957. Shown actual size $5\frac{1}{2} \times 5\frac{1}{2}$ in. (14×14 cm).

Martyrs and should be a sombre colour, whereas the red of Whitsun is a bright fiery colour. Green in all its hues gives promise for the future, fruitfulness, birth and hope, and is used from Trinity to Advent. Rose pink is used after Trinity and in the Roman Catholic Church it is used for the fourth Sunday in Advent and mid-Lent Sunday. Blue is for eternity, faith and truth, it is used for Advent and the first four weeks of Lent in the Church of England. Black is darkness and is used for funerals, sometimes for All Souls' Day and on Good Friday in the Roman Catholic

Church. Before attempting to make use of colour do seek advice. Mention the word 'lace' and the average person's thoughts fly straight to white and although you have mentally seen your design in colour it will have to be a stated fact before others see it the same way. Go armed with a painting of the design in the colours you intend to use, then use the painted design as well to match your threads.

Fig. 105
From very early history the Holy Spirit has been
represented by the dove. It is also an emblem for
peace. This very stylized design would be suitable
for a beginner as there are no curved lines to cause
problems over gaining or losing stitches.

Wheels being used as a cluster of grapes in a vine
design (right)

140

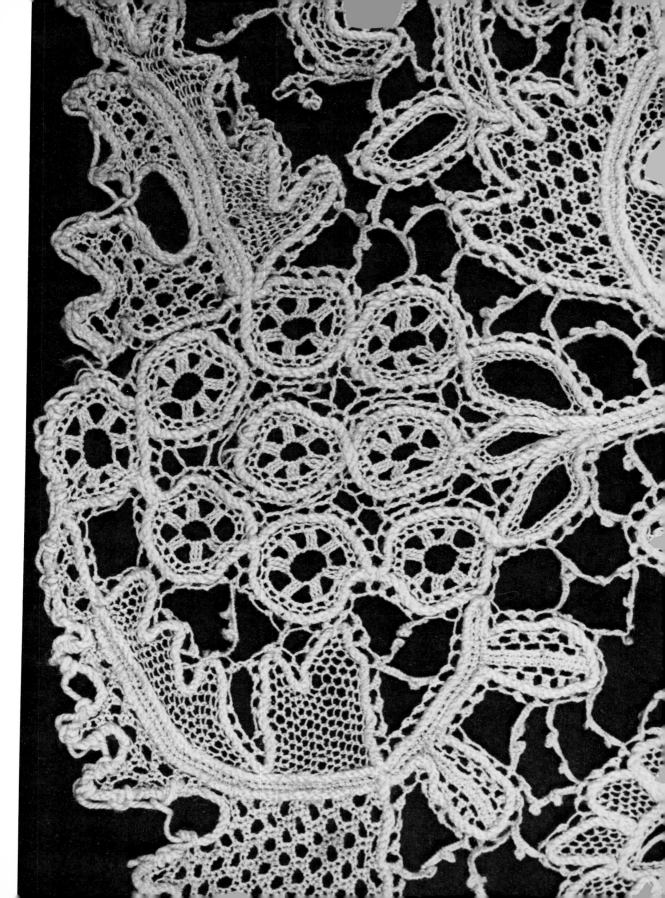

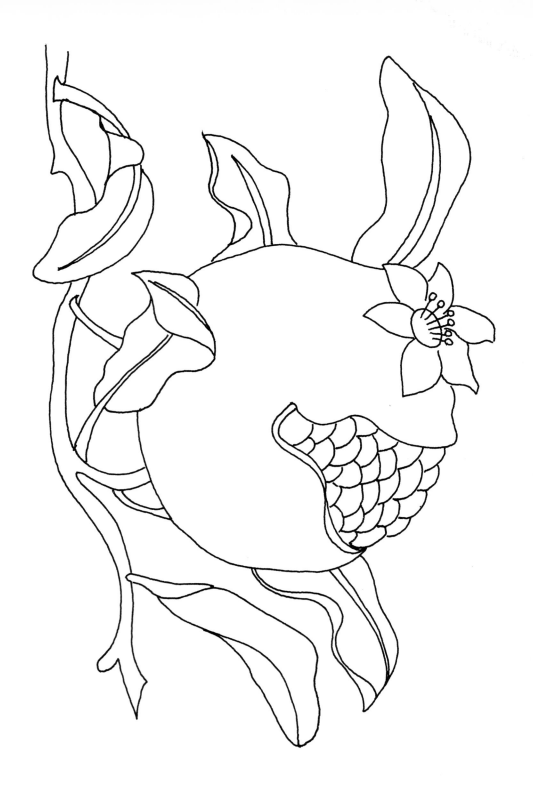

Lace is a fabric; to most people it is soft and flowing, very delicate, something that has to be treated with great care. Needlepoint lace is not like that, it does not have to edge garments unless that is the way it is intended to be used. If that is the case it can be made soft and pliable to hang in graceful folds. So this is another point that has to be stressed, if a strong, substantial, colourful fabric is needed for an altar cloth or frontal, or to decorate eucharistic vestments, needle-made lace can be that fabric.

The design will be made up of solid and open spaces; if, when finished, it is to be applied to a background material, do make sure that all areas are stab stitched through to the backing. Loose edges of the lace could be caught and pulled out of position by any moving object. This is not so likely to happen when the fabric is used as 'lace' as it is when applied and used in an embroidery.

Fig. 106
The pomegranate is a church symbol and represents the tree of life, shown with the seeds revealed, each seed a new growth, therefore proof of future life. Another meaning is the inner unity of countless seeds in one fruit, the Church.

SUPPLIERS

UNITED KINGDOM

D. J. HORNSBY, 149 High Street, Burton Latimer, Kettering, Northamptonshire. Threads, needles, pins, etc.

AUDREY SELLS, 49 Pedley Lane, Clifton, Shefford, Bedfordshire. Threads, pins, needles, Carrick-ma-Cross scissors, net.

KEN & PAT SCHULTZ, Ixworth Road, Honington, Nr Bury St Edmunds, Suffolk. Books, pillows, carrying cases

LEONIE COX, 9 St Peters Road, Twickenham TW1 1QY. Pure silks

JACK PIPER, Silverdale, Flax Lane, Glemsford, Suffolk CO10 7RS. Pure silks

THE ENGLISH LACE SCHOOL, St Peters Road, Tiverton, Devon. Books, threads, needles, pins

MACE & NAIRN, 89 Crane Street, Salisbury, Wiltshire. Books, needles, Carrick-ma-Cross scissors, net, threads

UNITED STATES OF AMERICA

LACIS, 2990 Adeline Street, Berkley, California 94703-2590. Books, threads, needles, pins, Battenberg tapes. Carrick-ma-Cross scissors

ZABEL ARAKELIAN, 29884 Muirland Drive, Garmington Hills, Michigan 48018. Custom-made pillows

ROBBINS BOBBINS, Rt 1 Box 294-1 Mineral Bluff, Georgia 30559. Custom-made pillows, linen, books

RICHARD GRAULICH, 5522 Sherrier Place N.W. Washington, DC 20016. Silk thread

INDEX